MW00986104

# CUTTING
## *to the*
# CORE

# CUTTING
## *to the*
# CORE

THE SEVEN COMPONENTS OF CHRISTIAN CHARACTER

## *Rick Ezell*

kregel
PUBLICATIONS

Grand Rapids, MI 49501

*Cutting to the Core: The Seven Components of Christian Character*

© 2001 by Rick Ezell

Published by Kregel Publications, a division of Kregel, Inc., P.O. Box 2607, Grand Rapids, MI 49501. For more information about Kregel Publications, visit our web site: www.kregel.com.

All rights reserved. No part of this book may be reproduced, stored in a retrieval system, or transmitted in any form or by any means—electronic, mechanical, photocopy, recording, or otherwise—without written permission of the publisher, except for brief quotations in printed reviews.

Unless otherwise noted, Scripture quotations are from the *Holy Bible, New International Version*®. © 1973, 1978, 1984 by International Bible Society. Used by permission of Zondervan Publishing House. All rights reserved.

Scripture quotations marked LB are from *The Living Bible*, © 1971 by Tyndale House Publishers, Wheaton, Illinois. Used by permission.

Scripture quotations marked NASB are from the *New American Standard Bible*. © the Lockman Foundation 1960, 1962, 1963, 1968, 1971, 1972, 1973, 1975, 1977.

Scripture quotations marked KJV are from the King James version of the Holy Bible.

Scripture quotations marked NEB are from *The New English Bible*. © The Delegates of the Oxford University Press and the Syndics of the Cambridge University Press 1961, 1970. Reprinted by permission.

Scripture quotations marked GNB are from the *Good News Bible*—Copyright © American Bible Society 1976; New Testament: Copyright © American Bible Society 1966, 1971, 1976.

Cover design: John M. Lucas

**Library of Congress Cataloging-in-Publication Data**
Ezell, Richard.
   Cutting to the core: the seven components of Christian character / Rick Ezell.
      p.     cm.
   1. Christian life—Baptist authors. 2. Character. 3. Bible. N.T. Peter, 2nd, I, 3–8—Criticism, interpretation, etc.
4. Christian life—Biblical teaching. 5. Character—Biblical teaching.
I. Title.
BV4501.3 .E64        2001        241—dc21        2001029022
                                                 CIP

ISBN 0-8254-2530-1

Printed in the United States of America

1 2 3 4 5 / 05 04 03 02 01

*To my daddy,*
*Hollis Coleman Ezell Sr. (1910–1982),*
*who, more than anyone I know,*
*lived a distinctive life of Christlike character.*

# CONTENTS

# ACKNOWLEDGMENTS

Many years ago, when I served on the staff of Emmanuel Baptist Church in Overland Park, Kansas, I was asked to lead a seminar on Christlike character at a youth ministry conference. It was suggested that I use 2 Peter 1:3–8 as the biblical basis for the seminar. Since that time I have repeatedly studied and taught, based upon this text, the formation of Christlike character.

Since my days in Overland Park, my journey has taken me to many places. I have visited parts of the world that I had only read about. I have encountered people who have touched and helped shape my life. I have witnessed the hand of God working in amazing ways. I have spoken at or participated in events for which only God knows why I was on the program. Each step of my journey reminds me of my need for living a distinctive, God-honoring life. My hope and prayer is that I have encouraged others to live a life of distinctive character.

The contents of this book have been filtered through many people. I have preached and taught its contents. My congregation, Naperville Baptist Church in Naperville, Illinois, has heard these thoughts in various forms since I became their pastor, and they have lived out these truths. Because of the transient nature of the congregation, it is my hope that they have taken these teachings to the ends of the earth.

I am thankful to Jan Porter and Pat Hill, who handle many of the administrative tasks of my job so that I am free to study and write; and to Carol Hendrickson, who has labored over the manuscript, proofreading and editing. Some great people work alongside of me as both paid and volunteer staff. I'm grateful to be a part of a team of men and women who seek to help people say *yes* to Jesus.

As always, I am reminded of God's mercy and grace through my wife, Cindy, and our daughter, Bailey. No words can express how they have tenderly touched and graced my life.

*His divine power has given us everything we need for life and godliness through our knowledge of him who called us by his own glory and goodness. Through these he has given us his very great and precious promises, so that through them you may participate in the divine nature and escape the corruption in the world caused by evil desires.*

*For this very reason, make every effort to add to your faith goodness; and to goodness, knowledge; and to knowledge, self-control; and to self-control, perseverance; and to perseverance, godliness; and to godliness, brotherly kindness; and to brotherly kindness, love. For if you possess these qualities in increasing measure, they will keep you from being ineffective and unproductive in your knowledge of our Lord Jesus Christ.*

*—2 Peter 1:3–8*

# INTRODUCTION

Character isn't inherited. One builds it <u>daily</u> by the
way one thinks and acts, thought by thought, action
by action. [1]

—Helen Gahagan Douglas

*[handwritten notes: Thought, Word, Deed/Action, Attitude, motive ♡]*

The most pressing need in our world today is <u>distinctive charac-</u>
ter—behavior based on high moral standards that don't succumb
to the whim of the moment or the dictates of the majority. This
trait is, unfortunately, in short supply and diminishing every day.
Without character you will not be the leader, the student, the
parent, the spouse, the man or woman whom God desires you
to be.

In *Character: America's Search for Leadership*, Gail Sheehy writes,
"The root of the word 'character' is the Greek word for engrav-
ing. As applied to human beings, it refers to the enduring marks
<u>left by life</u> that <u>set one apart as an individual</u>."[2] In other words,
character is that encompassing ingredient in one's life that makes
one different. Character embodies the <u>sum total of our being</u>
<u>and our actions</u>. It originates with who we are but expresses it-
self in the way we <u>live</u> and <u>behave</u>. It is who we are without the
medals and the diplomas and the titles.

In the movie *Cool Runnings*,[3] young Dareese has a vision for
the first Jamaican Olympic bobsled team. He discovers a picture
of Erwin Brister, an old friend of his father's, who was a two-time

gold-medal Olympian in bobsledding. But, Brister was disqualified from the Olympics for adding weight to the nose of his American bobsled, and his two gold medals were revoked.

Dareese finds the now alcoholic Brister and challenges him to mobilize and train the team; Brister accepts. On the night before their qualifying run, Dareese's curiosity gets the best of him. "Hey coach, I have to ask you a question. You don't have to answer it if you don't want to."

Brister responds, "You want to know why I cheated, right? I guess that's a fair question. You see, Dareese, I had to win. I made winning my whole life, and when you've made winning your whole life, you have to win no matter what."

"But coach, you had two gold medals. You had it all!"

Coach Brister looks contemplatively at Dareese and says, "Dareese, a gold medal is a wonderful thing, but if you are not enough without it, you will never be enough with it."

Today, many are advancing their careers, but few seem interested in building a sound character. All too frequently, who we are is sacrificed upon the altar of ambition and worldly success. But what we want to achieve is not nearly as important as what we become. It's possible to perform worthwhile activities yet not to be a person of authenticity. It's unfortunate, however, that people emphasize doing rather than being, accomplishment rather than character. Nothing is wrong with accomplishment, but who we are is more important than what we do. Many people, as Brister was, are so wrapped up in winning at a game or a profession that they forget to win at life.

The following pages examine the elements in 2 Peter 1:3–8 that constitute the core of distinctive character. In the Scripture passage, the apostle Peter lists seven characteristics that, once added to faith, will yield a character of distinction. These traits do not come automatically; they require hard work. None are optional; all must be integrated into the daily life of a Christian. While constructing the traits, they appear to build on each other.

But in developing these traits in our lives, we do not work on one trait then start on another; all are developed simultaneously. The end result is a character marked by distinction.

The first section, "The Start," consists of two chapters. They examine the divine dimensions that form the nucleus of character, and lay the foundation stone of faith, upon which the steps to a distinctive character are built.

The second section, "The Steps," contains seven chapters that delve into the seven components of resplendent character. Each component builds on the other, leading to the final and crowning component of character—love.

The final section, "The Secret," contains two chapters that provide the necessary tools for consistently displaying the life of distinctive character.

The task before you will not be easy, but it will be rewarding. Part of the work may at times be unpleasant as you are encouraged to take an honest look at yourself. But think of it as an adventure, one that leads you to a distinctive character that emulates the nature of God. I wish for you a life-changing quest.

# PART ONE

# The Start

*His divine power has given us <u>everything we need</u> for life and godliness through our knowledge of him who called us by his own glory and goodness. Through these he has given us his very great and precious promises, so that through them you may participate in the divine nature.*

*—2 Peter 1:3–4a*

# THE BARGAIN OF A LIFETIME

His divine power has given us <u>everything</u> we need for
life and godliness. . . .

—2 Peter 1:3

Talent develops in quiet places, character in the full
current of human life.[1]

—Johann Wolfgang Von Goethe

A lawyer in a small Southern town was asked to defend a young
black man who had been charged with attacking a white girl.
When he agreed to defend the young man, the lawyer immediately came under the abuse and scorn of the townspeople. The
boy was innocent, and the lawyer defended him capably; but
when the jury came in, nobody was surprised at the verdict—
guilty. The lawyer's two children were at the courthouse. Unable
to find seats downstairs, they had gone into the segregated balcony and sat next to the town's black preacher. As the judge retired, spectators filed out of the courtroom. Jean, the lawyer's
daughter, was engrossed in watching her father. <u>A beaten man
but with his soul intact,</u> he put on his coat and walked down the
middle aisle toward the exit. Jean felt someone touch her shoul-
der. She was reluctant to take her eyes off her father as he made
the lonely walk down the aisle.

"Miss Jean Louise?" She turned around and noticed that everyone in the balcony was standing. The black preacher said, "Miss Jean Louise, stand up. Your father's passin'."[2]

Atticus Finch, Harper Lee's fictional lawyer in *To Kill a Mockingbird*, is a man of character and integrity. *Stand up. Your father's passin'.* A quality, a nobility, something distinguished resides in this man. He rises above the crowd; he displays a character that differentiates him from the norm.

I wonder, will people stand up and take notice of me because of the life I live and the character I display? Will I rise above the crowd? Will a distinctive life be revealed when I am cut to the core?

## The Core of Character

The thing that causes people to notice me—really notice me— is not my clothing, my car, my house, my money, or anything in my external world. It is not something I can put on, create, work up, or buy. Rather, it is something deep within—at the core of my being—a divine dimension that dwells in the inner sanctum of my heart. This distinctive nature is composed of four elements.

### Life

At our second birth God gave us a spiritual, eternal life to complete our physical life. This life is not *bios*, the necessities of life, such as food, clothing, and shelter. This life is *zoe.* It's best defined as *life as God knows it.* The fullness of life that belongs to God is now ours. It is not a possession but rather an infilling or indwelling of sorts—God once again breathes life into us. This dynamic transforms our internal world, seeps through to our external world, and is evidenced by a change of behavior and conduct.

Jesus offered this life when he said, "I have come that they may have life *[zoe]*, and have it to the full" (John 10:10). As one early church father said, "He became what we are to make us what he is." We now have the ability to share the life of God—but only in Jesus Christ can that potential be realized.

I like to think of this life as an <u>upgrade.</u> On a business trip, I arrived at the rental car agency to pick up the Ford Escort I had reserved. The attendant said, "We're all out of Ford Escorts. Would you mind a Lincoln Towncar at no extra charge?"

*Would I mind?*

On another occasion, my wife and I were informed by the ticket agent at the airline, "We have overbooked this flight. You have been upgraded from your coach class seat to first class. Do you mind?"

*Do we mind?*

That's what God has done for us in Jesus Christ. When we enter into this new and exciting relationship with him, he up-grades our life. He moves us beyond the physical to a new dimension of life, one that is <u>abundant</u> while we remain on this planet and is <u>eternal</u> when we leave this sphere.

## Likeness

Originally a *character* was a mark or symbol used in writing or printing. In the printing process, the press was rolled over the characters, imprinting the paper. In the same way, God has impressed his likeness or character onto our very natures. God's likeness is a <u>reflection</u> of his character.

The great biblical scholar, Dr. F. B. Meyer put it this way: "We reflect. The beauty of his face glancing on ours will be mirrored, as a man's eye will contain a tiny miniature picture of what he is beholding. Then we will be changed. If you try to represent Jesus in your character and behavior, you will become <u>transfigured</u> into his likeness. Love makes like. Imitation produces assimilation."[3] God desires to make us like him. As we draw near to him, we see ourselves as we are, but we also see God as he is. As a result of seeing more clearly the truth of both God and ourselves, we have an overwhelming urge to become more and more like God. As we seek his truth, we allow him to live in us. His likeness—his character—begins to rub off on us.

## Glory

We share in his glory, too. A. T. Robertson defined glory as "the manifestation of the Divine Character in Christ."[4] In the splendor of love, the glory of God spreads its rays like the sun. God expressed his pure self in such fullness in Christ that the apostle John wrote, "We have seen his glory, the glory of the One and Only, who came from the Father, full of grace and truth" (John 1:14). Jesus' glory attracted people to him.

As the glory was manifested from God to Jesus, it has now been manifested from Jesus to all believers. We don't possess that glory, mind you. But we radiate it. Recall the account of Moses going before God to intercede for the people (Exod. 33–34).

> Moses said, "Now show me your glory." And the LORD said, . . . "You cannot see my face, for no one may see me and live." Then the LORD said, "There is a place near me where you may stand on a rock. When my glory passes by, I will put you in a cleft in the rock and cover you with my hand until I have passed by. . . . But my face must not be seen." (33:18–23)

When Moses returned from Mount Sinai "he was not aware that his face was radiant because he had spoken with the LORD" (34:29).

Like a glow-in-the-dark figure, Moses had no light of his own. But after standing near the most brilliant light in the universe, he glowed. His face was charged with the glory of God.

In like manner, God's glory affects our lives. We have been given the privilege of beholding God face to face in Christ. His glory in our hearts transforms us from within. A poem given to me by a friend describes it beautifully.

> We, like the moon have no light, no energy, no power.
> Yet, we, like the moon when touched by the Son—
> Cast his brilliance on the blackest of nights.

As we look more and more into Christ's face, we radiate more and more of his nature. "But we Christians have no veil over our faces; we can be mirrors that brightly reflect the glory of the Lord. And as the Spirit of the Lord works within us, we become more and more like him" (2 Cor. 3:18 LB).

## Excellence

God stands above all others in rank, merit, and virtue. The attribute of excellence permeates everything God is and does. He formed man according to his image and likeness, and one can't get any better than that. The life and work of Jesus personified excellence as well. Mark recorded a spectator's response, a summation of Jesus' work: "He has done everything well" (Mark 7:37).

This quality of excellence and the desire to be and do one's best has been implanted into the believer's soul. I have known of people who immediately gave up alcoholic drink after conversion. One man, upon giving his heart to Christ, began immediately improving his handwriting. He remarked, "All things must be done well for Christ, even the little things." Others have changed their attitudes. Still others have cleaned up their foul mouths. Employers treated their employees with greater dignity and respect. Once God enters a life, the believer shares the ambition to do all things extraordinarily. This desire permeates a believer's being and changes his or her actions, thus transforming his or her character.

We must remember that excellence is not perfection, but the pursuit of perfection. And pursuit is what Jesus had in mind when he said, "Be perfect, therefore, as your heavenly Father is perfect" (Matt. 5:48). Too, excellence is not being *the* best; it is becoming *your* best. Excellence is a process of becoming the best one can be in all areas of life. That process involves intense and continual effort, prompting a lifetime challenge that is all consuming.

The divine dimensions—life, likeness, glory, and excellence—that make up the nature of God also, then, make up the God "impressed" nature of believers. These dimensions are implanted in the core of a believer's being, and become the mark of a believer. These qualities provide energy for the believer to do God's will. And because they produce features that distinguish a believer from the rest of society, others take notice. The Christian's nature is in communion with Christ, but this divine nature is not possessed. Rather, it is continually shared.

In cutting to the core of a Christ-follower, then, these character traits are exposed:

- Life—abundant, full, and dynamic
- Likeness—a lifestyle pleasing to God
- Glory—the radiating love of God as revealed in Jesus
- Excellence—the quality of being and doing one's best

In comparison to the all-demanding standard God sets before us in the Scriptures, all other standards are lesser alternatives. Take, for instance, knowledge or success. These standards would be more attainable and easier ones by which to measure progress. But God's standard for our lives is his nature, his character, as revealed in his Son Jesus Christ. True, God's standard is exacting—it raises the bar for effective living—but it, to use a familiar phrase, builds character.

# The Principles for Character Development

God desires for us to emulate his character. But he knows the challenge that presents. Because he loves us, he does not leave us to struggle alone; he provides the means for sharing his character. Following are guideposts that will lead us to emulate it.

## *Our Perfect Goal*

God's stated purpose for every believer, regardless of his or her vocation or calling, is to transform redeemed sinners into Jesus' image. "And we know that in all things God works for the good of those who love him, who have been called according to his purpose" (Rom. 8:28). God's "good" business is making our lives conform to Jesus' character—his life, his likeness, his glory, his — excellence. When we submit to the lordship of Christ, we acknowledge God's destination for us. We look at life through God's eyes, and we see that the ultimate end of his actions in our lives is not securing our happiness, but building his character in us.

Achieving this purpose may not be pleasant, easy, or painless. A glance at the way the Father exposed the Son to the realities of life and death is a sufficient reminder that we can expect the same kind of process in our lives. The desired result is conformity to him. We are like a diamond in the rough. For clarity and color to shine through, God must chisel, cut, and polish our characters. God works in and through the circumstances of our lives for his purpose—that his character may shine through.

When we understand God's workings, then we can make sense of our dark and painful experiences. God's idea of spiritual maturity is quite different from ours. C. S. Lewis understood this principle.

> Imagine yourself as a living house. God comes in to rebuild that house. At first, perhaps, you can understand

what He is doing. He is getting the drains right and stopping the leaks in the roof and so on: you knew that those jobs needed doing and so you are not surprised. But presently He starts knocking the house about in a way that hurts abominably and does not seem to make sense. What on earth is He up to? The explanation is that He is building a quite different house from the one you thought of—throwing out a new wing here, putting on an extra floor there, running up towers, making courtyards. You thought you were going to be made into a decent little cottage: but He is building a palace. He intends to come and live in it Himself.[5]

God's methods are not ours, and his standards are much higher. Thus, we often ask *Why? Why the tragedy? Why the crisis? Why the hurt? Why the pain?* The right question, however, is *What?* *What are you teaching me in this painful experience, God? What can I do to grow through the tragedy?* God is not a vengeful, punishing, whimsical God who lacks feelings for the created. Like sunshine penetrating a crystal, God desires to radiate his character through us. "We also rejoice in our sufferings, because we know that suffering produces perseverance; perseverance, character; and character, hope. And hope does not disappoint us, because God has poured out his love into our hearts by the Holy Spirit, whom he has given us" (Rom. 5:3–5). Sometimes God has to get our attention, to turn the facets of our crystal toward his light so that his rays may shine through us.

Daryl, at age thirty-five, returned home to live with his parents. I had seen him at church for several Sundays, holding tightly to one of his parents' arms.

I learned that Daryl was going blind. But he exhibited a quality and demeanor that caused me to take notice. I wanted to get to know him so I invited him to lunch. Over pizza and soft drinks he told me his story. Daryl had been raised in church. Nevertheless, he had tried it all—drugs, alcohol, jobs, and women. His pursuit for satisfaction and happiness led him farther and farther away from God. While in Seattle, Washington, he discovered he was losing his vision. Most people would have lashed out at God, but Daryl was that rare man who, through this heartbreaking experience, saw God. God was hammering and chiseling at Daryl's life, fashioning him to resemble the Lord Jesus. The process wasn't comfortable or easy but the results were apparent.

I invited Daryl to share his story with the youth group of our church. As the young people listened in awe and wonder, I'll never forget how Daryl closed his talk. "I had to go blind before I could see God. I pray that what has happened to me will never happen to you. Unless," he paused for a moment to make sure everyone heard his final words, "that is what it takes for you to see God."

Daryl not only understood, but he also shared the purpose of God for his life. In Daryl's crisis, a <u>distinctive life</u> was <u>being forged</u> and welded. What happened to Daryl was not a fluke, a tragic accident befalling one of God's children. Daryl's experience was a part of God's overarching goal for him to <u>radiate a life of character.</u>

## Knowing the Destination Before the Journey Begins

One of the most misunderstood verses in the Bible applies to character development: "For those God foreknew he also predestined to be conformed to the likeness of his Son, that he might be the firstborn among many brothers" (Rom. 8:29). *To predestine* literally means "to prehorizon" or "to define in advance the limits." This God did in determining that those who are redeemed shall experience salvation to the ultimate in that they will be "like Jesus." This predestination of God is not predestination to faith but a decision on God's part that sharing in his being will be the ultimate end of salvation. In other words, God has determined the final result of our redemption. He knows where we are headed before we get there.

A weaver sits at her loom to fashion a beautiful tapestry. She knows beforehand what her final product will be. She has a good idea what design she plans to employ. But the creative process may take some unexpected turns. When she encounters a mistake she does not undo her days of labor. Instead, she utilizes the mistake to enhance her design. The result is a more beautiful weaving than expected.

To look at it another way, I may plan a trip by car from Chicago to Kansas City. I know the final destination, but the journey may include some twists and turns along the way. En route, I may get off the interstate to enjoy a Swedish or Norwegian settlement. Or I may change course to tour a historical site like Mark Twain's home or the Winston Churchill Memorial. The stops do not alter the final destination. They do, however, make the trip more beneficial and profitable.

In like manner, God knows our final destination—distinctive character. In the pursuit, he employs the mistakes and the altered courses of our lives to make a more beautiful character. But, for this tapestry to be woven, we need to allow him control of the final product. Submission is not difficult when we understand the love of God. God is the divine potter and we are malleable clay in his tender, artistic hands. God says, "Like clay in the hand of the potter, so are you in my hand" (Jer. 18:6). His work is not a casual, whimsical effort. He knows the final result. He knows beforehand how we are to look and what we will be like. As a builder of a house follows a blueprint in building a structure, so the divine builder follows a blueprint for our lives.

What do we do while God performs his artistry on our lives? We stand face to face, looking into the image of Jesus Christ as revealed in Scripture. The path leading to a distinctive character is made clear by getting personal with Jesus.

For a period of time during my college years, I questioned my faith. I had grown up in church, had felt God's calling, and was studying for the ministry. But I doubted. My faith seemed second-hand, lacking authenticity. Who was this Jesus and how did he affect the life of a twentieth-century collegian? I was challenged to read and reread, openly and honestly, the life of Christ in the Gospels.

While reading I prayed, "Jesus, if you are real, manifest yourself to me." Day by day I read. Through the eyes of the gospel writers I examined the person of Christ. Soon I felt I could talk to this person. I began to discover a caring and compassionate God. He wasn't dead as some of my professors believed. He wasn't cold and boring as some churches portrayed. He wasn't just a friend as some colleagues expressed. He was more, so much more. He was the God of truth who had taken up residence in my life. He was the supreme author of life who had given his life to me. He had filled me with energy to pursue his nature, and now I wanted to emulate him.

The process of emulation initiated a quest for knowing Christ and growing in his likeness. And through that quest he changed my life. It wasn't a sudden transformation. It was more like a metamorphosis. A slow, gradual revelation and corresponding character change took place. Later, I realized that God was conforming me to the image of Christ. As I stood face to face with him, looking into Scripture, the predetermined character was having a profound effect on me. The wheels turned in the right direction toward a life of distinction.

## An Inner Power

It is marvelous that Jesus not only demonstrates what life is; he also enables believers to live life as it ought to be lived. We do not take Christ merely as an external model; we receive him as an internal power. "His divine power has given us everything we need for life and godliness" (2 Peter 1:3). This power is an inherent power. It resides in us because the nature of God is in us, and

God's power cannot be defeated or destroyed. If we permit it, his power will <u>spark</u> the changes that lead to distinctive lives. God is not stingy. He is <u>lavish</u> in giving to his children all the equipment necessary for sharing in the life and likeness of God.

From where does this power come?

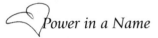

## Power in a Name

Believers are given the power "to become children of God" (John 1:12). Godly character can be ours because of *whose* we are not because of *who* we are. Certain privileges and rights have been granted to us because we are a part of God's family and share his name.

When I finished graduate school, I interviewed for a church staff position near my hometown in Alabama. The pastor conducted most of the interview. I had met him only once prior to this encounter, but he knew my sister and was acquainted with my father. Near the end of the interview he said, "Rick, one can't tell much about a person's character from a resume. But I know you are from good stock."

*I know you are from good stock*—those words made me realize the heritage that had been handed down to me from my parents. And I had the responsibility to uphold their good name. I also realized the power that this "good name" gave me to maintain it. The psychology of the pastor's statement motivated me to bring honor and respect to the Ezell name. I was from "good stock."

When we come to realize what God has given us through sharing his name, it should <u>inspire and impel</u> us to live righteous and blameless lives. We are from "good stock." Granted we have inherited a sin nature, but we have also been given a divine nature. We share in God's nature and are called by his name. Because of that relationship, we have the <u>responsibility, with his power,</u> to uphold his good name.

## Power in a Presence

God's power is not a once-and-for-all experience. The indwelling power of the presence of Christ through the Holy Spirit is always present, is ours daily. This power has, however, been ignored, misunderstood, and misused. By our ignorance and *ignore-ance* we have short-circuited the power of the Holy Spirit.

## Power from an Event

The power demonstrated through the resurrection of Jesus Christ is available to us as well. Paul wanted "to know Christ and the power of his resurrection" (Phil. 3:10). Paul prayed that the Ephesians would "begin to understand how incredibly great his power is to help those who believe him. It is that same mighty power that raised Christ from the dead and seated him in the place of honor at God's right hand in heaven" (Eph. 1:19–20 LB). The Greek word for power is *dunamis*. This is the root word for the English word "dynamite." The dynamite of God is the resurrection power of Jesus. Unlike the loud exploding power of today, this power is quiet. It works through us to bring life into lifeless situations. It brings hope to hopeless circumstances, joy where laughter and praise have deserted. This power encourages us throughout the quest for character. It accompanies us, impelling us to allow God to reveal his character through our lives. God gives us dynamite power—the power that changes destiny.

## A Guarantee

God gives us a guarantee, a promise that our characters can and will become resplendent. "Through these he has given us his very great and precious promises, so that through them you may participate in the divine nature" (2 Peter 1:4). A promise is an assurance given by one person to another. God's promises are great and valuable, and he displays them in his very character:

- God finishes what he starts: "Being confident of this, that he who began a good work in you will carry it on to completion until the day of Christ Jesus" (Phil. 1:6).
- God fashions us to perfection: "For we are God's workmanship, created in Christ Jesus to do good works, which God prepared in advance for us to do" (Eph. 2:10).
- God supplies our needs along the way: "And my God will meet all your needs according to his glorious riches in Christ Jesus" (Phil. 4:19).
- God gives us the strength we need for the trip: "I can do everything through him who gives me strength" (Phil. 4:13).
- God promises his presence on the journey: "My Presence will go with you, and I will give you rest" (Exod. 33:14).
- God promises comfort and rest when the course is painful: "Come to me, all you who are weary and burdened, and I will give you rest" (Matt. 11:28).

God has promised forgiveness to the sinful, rest to the weary, comfort to the sad, hope to the dying, and life to the dead, all for one reason—so that our characters reflect the image of Christ. The promises guarantee and confirm that we share in the very being of God. They assure us that we may escape the control of corruption and evil in the world and live a life that causes others to take notice. The Bible holds more than seven thousand promises. They are like a blank check, made out to us and signed by God, for the fulfillment of his predetermined plan and will.

It is unfortunate that we often don't take these promises to heart. We treat the promises like many people treat the items on display at the mall—they look but they don't buy. Oh, they admire and dream and wish, but they don't say, "I'll take it." Many believers treat God's promises identically. The great preacher, Vance Havner, eloquently expressed this misfortune.

> In the realm of things spiritual we have with us the Bible window-shopper. He moves along through the Book reading its precious promises, hearing its high challenges, and looking at its deep messages of peace and power and victory. But he never makes them his own. He appreciates but does not <u>appropriate</u>. He respects his Bible, argues for it, counts it dear, but its rich treasures never become living realities in his own experience. He is a window-shopper amongst the storehouses of God's revealed truth.[6]

All of the truths, riches, and promises of God are available to  us. The promises exist not simply for our scrutiny but for our sustenance. We are not merely to admire them and to occasionally quote them. We must enter the storehouse of God's Word and take the treasures as our own. We thereby appropriate the promises—<u>living out</u> the guarantees in our daily walk—for the purpose of revealing character.

When we become <u>inundated with God's Word we are transformed</u> and made distinctive. I love the story about the converted cannibal living in the South Sea Islands. As he sat by a large pot reading his Bible an anthropologist approached him and asked, "What are you doing?"

The native replied, "I'm reading the Bible."

The anthropologist scoffed and said, "Don't you know that modern, civilized man has rejected that book? It's nothing but a pack of lies. You shouldn't waste your time reading it."

The cannibal looked him over from head to toe and replied, "Sir, if it weren't for this book, you'd be in that pot!"

God's Word had changed his life as well as his appetite.

Those who are serious about their character conforming to

Christ's character will know the promises and will take those
promises to heart. And those promises will change your life, too.

## Share the Being of God

One word in this chapter puts God's being, his character, within
my reach and yours. The word is *share*. It is used a lot these days,
especially in transmitting information. People who come to speak
say they have come to share. One definition of *share* in *The American Heritage Dictionary of the English Language* is "to participate in,
use, enjoy, or experience jointly or in turns, to relate to another or
others; to have a share or part."[7] The biblical word for sharing,
*koinonia*, means to take part or share, to have some of the qualities
or attributes of something. Fellowship is the common translation
for *koinonia*. All too often fellowship means cookies and punch
after church. But that's not what the biblical writers had in mind.
At the heart of their concept was the giving and receiving of all
each possesses. It implies walking in the other person's shoes, experiencing life with empathy for the other. That's what God wants
for us and from us. The *Shorter Catechism* asks, "What is the chief
end of man?" It answers, "The chief end of man is to glorify God
and to enjoy Him forever." We can't enjoy God nor can God enjoy
us unless we participate in life together. I must submit to God and
say, "God, here is my life. I give it to you." God in return responds,
"Here is my life. It is yours." A sharing, a comradeship, a bonding
occurs. And that makes life peaceful and worth living. It also brings
distinctive character to fruition.

God has explained his purpose, expressed his predestination,
unveiled his power, and given his promises for one reason—so
that you and I might become partners in his nature. The apostle
Peter explains, "so that through them you may participate in the
divine nature" (2 Peter 1:4). Or, as the *New English Bible* translates this phrase, "come to share in the very being of God."

Do you see what God has been saying all along? "What you

have and what you are—your being—and what I have and what
I am—my being—we will share, we will participate in, we will
use, we will experience together in common."

In *Come Share the Being*, Bob Benson reminds us of an old-
fashioned Sunday school picnic.

> Do you remember when they had
>     old fashioned Sunday school picnics?
> It was before air-conditioning.
>     They said, "We'll meet at Sycamore Lodge
> in Shelby Park at 4:30 Saturday.

You bring your supper and we'll furnish the tea."

But you came home at the last minute
    and when you got ready
to pack your lunch,
    all you could find in the refrigerator
was one dried up piece of baloney
    and just enough mustard in the bottom of the jar
so that you got it all over your knuckles
    trying to get to it.
And there were just two stale pieces of bread.
    So you made your baloney sandwich
and wrapped it in some brown bag
    and went to the picnic.

And when it came time to eat
    you sat at the end of a table and spread
out your sandwich.
    But the folks next to you—the lady was a good cook
and she had worked all day
    and she had fried chicken, and baked beans,
and potato salad, and homemade rolls,
    and sliced tomatoes,

and pickles, and olives, and celery,
   and topped it off with
two big homemade chocolate pies.
   And they spread it all out beside you
and there you were with your baloney sandwich.

But they said to you,
   "Why don't we put it all together?"
"No, I couldn't do that, I just couldn't even think of it,"
   you murmured embarrassedly.
"Oh, come on, there's plenty of chicken
      and plenty of pie, and plenty of everything—
    and we just love baloney sandwiches.
     Let's just put it all together."
   And so you did and there you sat
    eating like a king
    when you came like a pauper.[8]

God offers you something like that. The bargain of a lifetime—
to share with God. I have so little to offer and God has so much
to give. I am weak and he is strong. I am sinful and he is holy. All
I have is a baloney sandwich and he has a feast. It doesn't seem
right. It isn't right; it is an act of love.

Yet when we take up God's offer to share, a transformation
occurs. The unveiling of a new life takes place. A noticeably different life emerges. A life that causes people to stand up and take
notice.

*Chapter 2*

# THE FOUNDATION OF FAITH

For this very reason, make every effort to add to your faith. . . .

—2 Peter 1:5

Faith is the daring of the soul to go farther than it can see.[1]

—William Newton Clarke

I watched the process with fascination. My second-story office window provided an unobstructed view of the work site for the construction of a new educational wing on the church. Each day the skill of the crew and the progress of their work filled me with awe and wonder.

I was most amazed, though, by the great care the workers put into preparing the soil for the foundation. The day after the groundbreaking ceremonies the bulldozer excavated the land. When finished, the ground lay smooth as glass. Next, onto the smooth dirt a dump truck poured a gray, chalky substance—a mixture of fine gravel and chemicals. The workmen spread and smoothed the mixture, forming a second layer. Then the workers outlined the dimensions of the foundation with posts and string. Simultaneously, the plumbing contractor laid and connected pipes for the water and sewer lines. Finally, a frame of steel and wood formed the boundaries for the poured concrete.

From the initial day to the pouring of the foundation, over a month elapsed. I couldn't believe it was taking so long. The work crew labored diligently and continually for over twenty days, preparing the foundation.

Proper preparation is mandatory. Without the necessary groundwork a structure is weak and precarious. Although the preparations are often hidden and unnoticed they are, nevertheless, essential. A friend of mine used to say, "Proper preparations prevent poor performance."

As the foundation of a building is essential for structural integrity, a foundation of faith is essential in the development of a distinctive character. Faith in Christ is the necessary ingredient that makes one a believer. Faith is the first step that begins the journey of the Christ-follower toward the destination of distinctive character. Faith has many definitions and countless synonyms. But for the development of character, faith can be defined as the opening of our hearts to what Christ has to give—his nature and being—and yielding our lives to what he desires—a godly character.

## A Picture of Faith

I love to snow ski. No other sport thrills and invigorates me as does slicing through the powder down the face of a mountain. Surveying the beauty of God's creation from a mountaintop is a breathtaking experience. On one particular outing I witnessed one of the most astonishing and humbling displays of faith that I had ever seen—a blind skier! Clad in orange, the skier sliced down the side of the mountain with his guide close behind. As they glided down the hill in tandem, the instructor barked out instructions. "Left," shouted the instructor, and the blind skier sliced to the left. The instructor shouted, "Right," and the blind skier followed the command. As other commands were given by the instructor the blind skier obeyed, and together they maneuvered the slope, avoiding trees, people, and moguls, while experiencing the thrill and exhilaration of downhill skiing.

As I watched, my eyes watered. I had witnessed faith in its truest form. The blind skier was yielding and obedient to his instructor; in return, he experienced the joy of skiing. Likewise, yieldedness and joy are the essence of faith for the believer in Christ.

Faith allows us to experience all that Christ has to give—his life, his likeness, his glory, and his excellence. Returning to the foundation analogy, faith is the bedrock that supports the construction of distinctive character.

People demonstrate faith every day. A woman enters a restaurant, for example, sits in a chair she has never sat on, orders food from a waiter she has never seen before, eats food prepared by a cook she has never met. The entire episode occurs by faith. It takes faith to get a prescription filled, faith to deposit money in a bank, sign a contract, drive on a highway, or get on an airplane. Faith, then, isn't always a religious experience.

Faith is only as effective as its object. If we trust money, we get what money can do; if we trust ourselves, we get what we can do; if we trust God, we get what he can do. And what can God do? He can transform us into people who reflect his being, and it is this result that makes the Christian's faith different.

The foundation of faith for the Christ-follower consists of three essential ingredients. As we move toward a life of distinctive character these essentials—commitment, obedience, and action—sustain us along the way.

## Faith Debuts in Commitment

Faith for the Christian is more than merely believing that there is a God. James 2:19 informs us that even the demons believe in God. In the New Testament, faith is expressed by commitment to a person, that is, committing one's all to the person of Jesus Christ. The Philippian jailer asked Paul and Silas, "What must I do to be saved?"

(Acts 16:30). Paul answered, "Believe in the Lord Jesus, and you will be saved" (v. 31). The jailer knew that Paul meant that he needed to entrust his life to Jesus as master, mediator, and Messiah.

Jesus did not call for a halfhearted trust. When the rich young ruler sought to follow him, the Master exhorted, "One thing you lack. . . . Go, sell everything you have and give to the poor, and you will have treasure in heaven. Then come, follow me" (Mark 10:21). Jesus does not ask for a partial commitment. With him it is all or nothing.

Faith—faith that saves—entails the complete surrender of one's life to Christ. A partial faith doesn't make sense. A contradiction occurs when one says, "I sort of believe." One either believes or doesn't believe. Without a total surrender of all that one knows about oneself to all that one understands about Jesus, there is no faith.

A story tells about a man who walked along the edge of a steep embankment. Stepping onto loose rocks, the traveler lost his footing, slipped, and plummeted down the cliff. As luck would have it, a branch protruded from the face of the mountain, and the hapless man grabbed hold.

Catching his breath, he looked up and called out, "Is anyone up there?"

A voice replied, "Yes. My name is Jesus."

"Will you help me?" the man pleaded.

"Yes, but first you must let go," Jesus commanded.

After a long pause the man called out, "Is anyone else up there?"

I told that story once to a group of high school students at a winter retreat. When I concluded, a teenage girl in the back of the room said, "Why don't you finish the story?"

"But that's all I know," I said. "You tell how it ends."

"Well," she started, "the man fell down the mountainside just before daybreak. Within minutes following the conversation with Jesus, the sun peaked over the horizon. At that moment the man realized he was only a few feet from the bottom."

Beautiful ending, isn't it? But, imbedded within the story is a more fascinating truth. I once heard Ann Kiemel describe faith as "jumping out of an airplane at thirty thousand feet without a parachute knowing that God will catch you. If he doesn't, you splatter!" And then she added, "But how do you know unless you jump?"

Faith is letting go of all that we have and are to the complete charge and authority of Christ, and knowing that he will be there for us with all that he has and is. Faith is a complete confidence in the nature of God. He is who he says he is, and he does what he has promised. God provides, protects, and launches you into a new life. That we can count on.

A life of character emerges from a complete trust in the person of Christ. How could we submit all areas of our lives if we did not trust him? When we trust Christ we expose for examination and renovation the deepest, most vulnerable aspects of our being to the tender and loving hands of our Savior. A life of <u>continual</u> commitment to the person of Christ constitutes the first step in laying the foundation for building a life of Christlike character.

## Faith Develops Through <u>Obedience</u>

As we build on our foundation of faith we realize that God wants the best for us. The divine architect of our lives is a loving heavenly Father. He is not a demonic dictator seeking to punish and to inflict pain and suffering on his subjects. Instead, he is the <u>infinite lover.</u> The one who created us. The one who accompanies us. The one who prepares a fantastic future for us.

We <u>thus respond in obedience.</u> A law of physics states that for every action there is an equal and opposite reaction. As God demonstrates his loving action toward us we respond with an equal action of obedience toward him. Without the reaction—the corresponding obedience—faith is incomplete, and it will wither and die.

When the Philippian jailer arose from his knees after believing in Jesus he knew what was expected. He then entered a life of obedience. "At that hour of the night the jailer took them [Paul and Silas] and washed their wounds; then immediately he and all his family were baptized" (Acts 16:33). Note that, in obedience, the jailer began serving others, was baptized, and sought to bring others into a relationship with Christ. In the New Testament, belief and obedience are not separate concepts. Rather they are united in one word—*faith.* Belief impels a commitment to full obedience; obedience, therefore, is not simply an option.

A lifestyle of *dis*obedience, however, eats relentlessly at our faith. Disobedience often means taking the easy way out, relying on our own understanding rather than God's. When we fail to obey, our trust muscles get little exercise and grow flabby.

When we obey we discover that God is trustworthy. And that trustworthiness is felt at a deep level. It's no longer a head knowledge; it's a heart and soul knowledge. As Corrie ten Boom expressed, "The older I get the less I question and the more I trust."[2] That's the posture arrived at through obedience; faith grows through exercising obedience.

It is interesting that Jesus never told his disciples, "Believe me." He always exhorted, "Follow me." He expected loyalty then, and he is looking for it now—a loyalty based on love. Supreme obedience has always been translated as an expression of love. Christ loves us. We, in turn, love him.

Once the foundation of faith with Christ is laid, then a whole new relationship is built. We become obedient to him not because we have to but because we want to. No longer do we fear the Master, but a loving affection emerges and grows.

In *Faith Is for People,* Paul Little illustrates the transformation that takes place in the life of a housekeeper who is hired by a wealthy businessman. He hires her and says, "Now look, I'm paying you a hundred dollars a week. Here is a list of forty things I want you to accomplish. I expect you to finish the list by the end of the week." The housekeeper is getting paid to do these things, so she does them.

But suppose that this housekeeper and this businessman fall in love and are ultimately married. He drives off to work and leaves no list. His friends scold him, "You're crazy! No list? She'll sit with her feet up on the table all day long, watching television and eating chocolates. The house will be a shambles. You're crazy. You better get her back on that list."

But the businessman replies, "No, you don't understand. I don't need to give her a list. She will now accomplish sixty things with no list." Why? Because the woman is no longer just a hired house-keeper, but is a wife who loves her husband. A whole new relation-ship has developed. The list is no longer necessary. A relationship built on obedience alone has been transformed by love.[3]

This change, or conversion, is precisely what happens in the life of a believer. Belief blooms into obedience because of the pollen of love. Obedience is our response to what God has done for us in his Son, Jesus Christ. When we acknowledge God's love, our relationship with him develops and matures.

This life-changing faith, however, develops because of a first-hand encounter with Christ. Many faithless people are disgruntled with God and his church. The reason? At one time they entered into a relationship with an institution—the church—but not with a living person—Christ. When we encounter and experience the vivacity and loveliness of Christ we respond in loving obedience. Our desire is to please and honor him through the development of our characters.

## Faith Is Displayed by Action

Action is the expression of faith. Faith is never passive or static, nor is it a certain feeling. Real faith always necessitates action. James, the brother of Jesus, wrote, "Faith by itself, if it is not accompanied by action, is dead. But someone will say, 'You have faith; I have deeds.' Show me your faith without deeds, and I will show you my faith by what I do" (James 2:17–18). James knew that dynamic faith rolls up its sleeves and gets to work.

Faith is best understood not as something you *have* but as something you *do*. When you only *have* faith, it can become inert. Rather than doing the job, you may find it easier to say, "I have faith that the job will get done." That kind of faith is an excuse for not doing the will of God, and it prevents you from experiencing the loveliness of Christ and the hope of the Holy Spirit. When faith is something you *do*, it provides the means and the ability for you to display a distinctive life through action.

Often we hear statements such as, "She has lots of faith," or "He doesn't have much faith," or "I wish I had more faith." But does faith come in sizes? The disciples thought so. "The apostles said to the Lord, 'Increase our faith!' He replied, 'If you have faith as small as a mustard seed, you can say to this mulberry tree, "Be uprooted and planted in the sea," and it will obey you'" (Luke 17:5–6). Jesus said nothing about increasing the size of faith or feeling you have the right amount of faith. He maintained that the tiniest bit of faith can do the impossible. Jesus selects the mustard seed as an object lesson for faith. The seed contains the germ of life. Yet it remains useless until planted. A miracle happens when the seed enters the soil. Under favorable conditions, the seed sprouts into a tree of majestic grace. Jesus is saying that action, not just feeling or thought, is what matters. The size of faith does not matter. Our attitude toward faith does not matter. That faith is acted upon is what matters.

Consider three men standing beside a frozen river. They all need to cross to the other side. The first says he doesn't believe the ice will hold, so he gives up and sits in the snow. The second says he'll step out on faith, then lies on the ice and crawls across, trembling the whole way. The third yells, "It'll hold!" He pulls up his dogsled and roars across the frozen stream like a locomotive, passing the second man in a flash.

Who displayed faith that the ice would hold? Both the one who roared across and the one who crawled.

Who did not? The one who sat in the snow—right?

But who had the *most* faith? It appears that the third man did. But the last two men both arrived at the same destination. True, one arrived faster and with less anxiety. But the real difference lies between the person who didn't possess faith and the ones who did. For those who expressed faith, the results were the same.

A suitable foundation for a life of character, then, isn't more faith, but the right kind of faith—a dynamic and vigorous belief in the resurrected Christ. Not a once-and-for-all, static act of acceptance, not an I'm-finished-and-that's-all-I-need kind of belief, but a living and growing confidence that penetrates all of life.

## Strengthening Faith

As we live out our faith, people, events, and circumstances will attempt to erode this foundation. The foundation of faith will weaken unless we give it the proper maintenance. Faith needs to be constantly strengthened and supported. Like the foundation was critical to the new church building, the foundation of faith is vital to the structure of a distinctive character. Character emerges in direct proportion to the strength of the foundation of faith.

How can our faith be fortified to withstand the attacks of forces that would seek to destroy it?

First, look at the Author of faith. We are instructed to "fix our eyes on Jesus, the author and perfecter of our faith" (Heb. 12:2). As the originator of the very idea of faith, Jesus also carries it through to completion. It only stands to reason that the more we know Jesus the greater our confidence in stepping out in faithful obedience.

Peter walked on the water knowing Jesus was present. The four men who lowered their friend through the thatch roof to Jesus had seen the miracle-man work. It was not enormous faith that enabled these people to accomplish great things. It was gazing at the person of Christ then acting upon what they saw.

As we are exposed to more of God's character and attributes, our faith will strengthen. Prayer, Bible studies, and worship are essential to effective faith. "Faith comes from hearing the message, and the message is heard through the word of Christ" (Rom. 10:17). A consistent time with God is essential for powerful faith. The more we learn of Christ and his role in our lives, the better we trust him.

A second way to fortify faith is by following the examples of faith. Football legends are enshrined in Canton, Ohio. Basketball greats live on in Springfield, Massachusetts. The cracks and thuds of baseball immortals echo in Cooperstown, New York. These various Halls of Fame dot our land, honoring all sorts of sports heroes. The Bible has a Hall of Fame, too. The author of Hebrews wrote in chapter 11 about men and women who demonstrated a remarkable faith throughout biblical history. Moses, David, and others are recorded as sources of encouragement and example. Their lives of faith should be examined thoroughly.

History offers other examples. The biographies of great men and women of God should be required reading for all Christians, especially those who want their faith strengthened. William Carey, the first modern missionary, traveled to India. His mission work started schools, churches, and translated the Bible into many languages and dialects. He was a great man of faith.

George Mueller, a pastor in England during the eighteenth century, lived by faith. He founded orphanages that cared for the neglected children of England. During his lifetime 7.5 million dollars was raised to educate 123,000 students and support 189 missionaries. He never made a plea, or sent out a brochure, or had a direct mail campaign. He was a man of faith who acted on what needed to be done and trusted in God for all of his needs.

John Wesley, the founder of Methodism, exemplified faith in action. He preached a total of 42,400 sermons, an average of fifteen per week for fifty-four years. He traveled 290,000 miles in his lifetime on foot or horseback, which is equal to encircling the globe over twenty times. His prolific writing included over two hundred volumes. When he died at the age of eighty-eight, Wesley left behind a worn coat, a battered hat, a humble cottage, a tattered Bible—and the Methodist church. Truly, he was an example of faith in action.

When you die what will you leave behind?

Space doesn't permit me to write about such heroes of faith as Billy Sunday, Dwight L. Moody, Billy Graham, and Corrie ten Boom, to name just a few. And unsung heroes of faith still surround us, if we will only notice. People of faith leave clues from their walk with God.

A Sunday school teacher I had as a teenager, for example, had survived disappointment and pain but still possessed an exciting faith. Why? She rose daily at 5:00 A.M. to spend two undisturbed hours with the Lord. She put into practice principle number one—look at the Author of faith. She always sat in the second pew from the front at church because she didn't want to be distracted. She took voracious notes because she wanted to grow and learn. To this day, she remains a vibrant encourager and stirring example of faith.

A third way to fortify your faith is to take a risk. Faith is not faith if it is not on the cutting edge of challenge and adventure. To dare is to live by faith. Anything short of that is a masquerade. Living as Christ desires but simultaneously playing it safe is impossible. Faith presumes risk.

An old pump offered the only hope of drinking water on a very long and seldom-used trail across the Amargosa Desert. The following note was found in a baking powder can wired to the pump handle.

This pump is all right as of June 1932. I put a new sucker washer into it and it ought to last five years. But the washer dries out and the pump has got to be primed. Under the white rock I buried a bottle of water, out of the sun and corked end up. There's enough water in it to prime the pump, but not if you drink some first. Pour about one fourth and let her soak to wet the leather. Then pour in the rest medium fast and pump like crazy. You'll git water. The well has never run dry. Have faith. When you git watered up, fill the bottle and put it back like you found it for the next feller.—Desert Pete

PS: Don't go drinking up the water first. Prime the pump with it and you'll git all you can hold.[4]

Faith is risky business. For faith to grow we must venture beyond our own abilities and resources. Out on a limb, doing the impossible, we test the resources of God and depend totally on him. Faith is always costly. But people of faith have learned to give all they have to God, and they trust him to give back all that they need. That's scary. But it's the only way for our faith to flourish.

By exercising our faith we take a risk. As we lay our faith on the line, God is unleashed to work in our lives. We must act even when it means asking for forgiveness when we have wronged someone, or tithing when we don't have the money to buy groceries, or quitting a job because of our convictions, or taking a stand for justice. If faith is not "up and doing," it atrophies. Muscles that aren't continually exercised become weak. So, too, a faith that does not walk becomes too weak to stand. To build muscle on our faith, every chance we get we should exercise our faith, daring to risk.

The fourth way to fortify faith is to expect results from your faithful action. Seeing God work is a great faith motivator. We can be challenged to believe, to follow examples, and to exercise our faith, but if we never see anything happen, we will soon give up. So look for and expect God to work when you walk in faith.

A huge maple tree grew in my mother's yard. As a kid I played around this tree. But in the past few years it had shown no signs of life. It was dead and had to be cut down. My mother got several estimates: five hundred to seven hundred and fifty dollars. At the same time, my mother's church had purchased a new organ. The church asked members to help pay for the organ by buying a key at two hundred and fifty dollars. Mother wanted to help finance the organ, but the cost of having the tree cut down loomed over her. What was she to do? She struggled with this decision for several days. Finally she decided, on faith, that she would give to the organ fund and expect God to provide for the removal of the dead tree.

On the Monday after she gave her check for the organ, mother returned home from a trip to find men in her yard looking at the rotten maple tree. The men were from the electrical department. They had noticed that the tree, if it fell, would pose a danger to the electrical lines. They wanted to cut it down. The workers asked if they could return the next day and not only cut down the tree, but also haul off the wood—all at no cost to my mother!

When we step out on faith, God works and provides results. William Carey, the cobbler who became the first missionary, said, "Expect great things from God; attempt great things for God."[5] Faith is not believing God *can* do wonders. It is believing God *will*. We limit God when we don't expect results.

A fifth way to fortify faith is to supplement it. I'm not advocating faith plus works for salvation. But I am saying that we need to pursue certain qualities for our faith to be functional and effective. The apostle Peter advocated reinforcing our faith with certain qualities. "For this very reason, make every effort to add to your faith goodness; and to goodness, knowledge; and to knowledge, self-control; and to self-control, perseverance; and to perseverance, godliness; and to godliness, brotherly kindness; and to brotherly kindness, love" (2 Peter 1:5–7). Faith is the room in which we live. But we furnish that room with the virtues of goodness, knowledge, self-control, perseverance, godliness, brotherly kindness, and love. Putting it another way, faith resembles a basic food group on which we live, but we supplement that diet with the vitamins and minerals we need for full health and vitality.

Just as God was lavish in giving us his promises and power, we must be lavish in adding the necessary qualities for the emergence of a distinctive, resplendent character. The word translated *add* or *supply* (NASB) in 2 Peter 1:5 has its origin in the elaborate plays of ancient Greece. Wealthy individuals trained, equipped, maintained, and supplied the chorus at their own expense. The Greek word thus conveys the idea of lavishness. It never means to equip in a miserly way. It means to pour out abundantly everything that is necessary for a great performance. Likewise, the believer is to lavishly supply all the necessary components in constructing a distinctive life.

In the remaining pages of this book you will become acquainted with these components. But, more importantly, you will discover steps for putting each component into practice, thus creating a life of distinctive character.

Faith is the foundation of that life, but a foundation is useless if no structure is built upon it. The believer supplies these components, adding one upon the other, building a resplendent character. And with faith as the foundation, love will be the capstone.

# PART TWO

# THE STEPS

*For this very reason, make every effort to add to your faith goodness; and to goodness, knowledge; and to knowledge, self-control; and to self-control, perseverance; and to perseverance, godliness; and to godliness, brotherly kindness; and to brotherly kindness, love.*

—2 Peter 1:5–7

*Chapter 3*

# BEING MORAL IN
# AN IMMORAL WORLD

. . . Add to your faith goodness. . . .

—2 Peter 1:5

No real excellence in the entire world can be separated from right living.

—Author Unknown

Ken appeared preoccupied as we lunched together in a restaurant. He had just finished leading a management seminar for a group of church leaders. After we discussed the seminar, our conversation centered on his business. The company where he served as executive vice-president was in Chapter 11 bankruptcy. A frantic effort was being made by the owner to sell the company before the bank foreclosed on a multimillion-dollar note. In the process of selling, many unscrupulous deals and unethical cover-ups were being made. These actions considerably troubled Ken.

Ken's ethical tension was heightened after he talked with a local community leader. Ken expressed to the community leader that even though he worked for this company, he did not agree with all the current practices nor did he participate in the underhanded schemes. The community leader replied, "A lot of people look at you as the number two man in the company and wonder if you aren't just like the owner. They want to know where you stand." Ken then realized that the community was scrutinizing his morality.

This dilemma, along with other concerns, led Ken to resign his position. His integrity was of greater importance than a job or status. It did not matter that some of the shady dealings were accepted in the business world. Nor did it matter that the other top managers were involved in the cover-up. But it did matter that Ken's reputation and integrity remain intact. He wanted his friends and his community to know that his character was not for sale.

One of the most difficult things we do on a day-to-day basis is to choose morality when the rest of society accepts immorality. To represent the facts when the management wants you to "fudge" the numbers in order to protect a poor judgment by the company. To stand by the truth when others stretch the truth of their products in order to make a sale. To reveal the actual data while some people inflate expense reports. To be honest when others choose to falsify records and lie to their advantage. To honor the company's time although others abuse sick leave policies and other employee benefits. To state income and disbursements correctly even though others blatantly cheat on personal income tax forms. To honor marriage by abstaining from premarital or extramarital affairs.

The life that exhibits distinctive character is different. Christ was different and he calls his followers to rise above the crowd. He calls us to be separate from the world, to take him seriously, and to respond appropriately to his teachings. Jesus calls his believers to be moral in an immoral world.

## Become an Expert at Living

After the proper foundation of faith is laid, the initial step in constructing a life of distinctive character begins with what the

Bible calls *goodness or moral excellence.* This virtue is where right belief—faith—is transformed into right actions—morality. Peter commanded, "Add to your faith goodness" (2 Peter 1:5). The *New American Standard Bible* translates this phrase "in your faith supply moral excellence." The Greek word for goodness or moral excellence, *arete,* is seldom used in the New Testament and not easily translated into our language. Translators often express its meaning with words such as *virtue, goodness, excellence,* or *praise.* The truth is *arete* means those things and more. *Arete* was often used of fertile land ready for planting. The land was free of rocks and weeds, and the soil was pure and rich. The land was ready to fulfill its purpose.

In reference to humankind, *arete* is that virtue that makes a person an expert in the technique of living, a person who is virtuous and pure. Any dross or impurities have been extracted or are at least in the process of being removed. That person is committed to goodness and holiness and, therefore, separated from sin. He or she is consecrated to God, always ready to show *whose* he or she is and *whom* he or she serves. That person is consistent in thinking as God thinks and desiring what God desires.

Understand—goodness is not equated simply with abstinence from certain acts, such as smoking, drinking, or dancing. Nor is it merely a particular style of dress or mannerism. Instead, the believer seeks to live in conformity to the moral precepts of the Bible and in contrast to the sinful ways of the world.

Morality is not optional for the Christ-follower. It is not an elective but a required subject—the major undertaking of a believer committed to character building. Morality is the everyday business of every Christian, and it evidences itself in the way we live hour by hour.

God's Word is clear on our pursuit of moral excellence:

> What sort of people ought you to be? Surely men of good and holy character . . . (2 Peter 3:11 PHILLIPS)

Make every effort to be found spotless, blameless and at peace with him. (2 Peter 3:14)

Just as he who called you is holy, so be holy in all you do. (1 Peter 1:15)

Live such good lives among the pagans that, though they accuse you of doing wrong, they may see your good deeds and glorify God on the day he visits us. (1 Peter 2:12)

God commands us to live lives that are different, set apart from the ordinary. Lives that are pure, blameless, righteous, and honorable. This manner of life will pervade all our beings as we strive for godly character.

Consider the following questions: Are your values and goals in life markedly different from those of your neighbors? Does  the use of your time, money, and energy reflect that difference? Is there anything distinctive about what you teach your children? Is your behavior different from that of your colleagues at work or at school? If there is nothing distinctive about your life, why go to the bother of being a Christian? At the heart of anyone bearing the name Christian is the desire to live a life that is distinct from the world.

A story, reportedly true, tells about a young man serving in the army of Napoleon. This man was extremely immoral, known for his foul mouth, his loose living, and his disrespect of others. The lewd man was brought before the emperor, who asked, "Are all the things that I have heard about you true?" Embarrassed, the young soldier replied, "Yes, Sir." Before pronouncing sentence, the emperor asked his name. "Napoleon," the young man answered softly. The emperor's eyes raged with fury. The emperor turned to the young man and commanded, "Either change your conduct or change your name!"

# The Epitome of Depravity

Why is living a moral life so difficult? Why do Christians conform to the world around them rather than to God? There are four reasons why believers are constantly defeated in their struggle with sin.

The first reason that people struggle with morality is because they fail to understand the holiness of God. Sinclair Ferguson described the holiness of God as "the total integrity of his being."[1] God is the epitome of moral excellence. He is different, set apart, unique, one of a kind. God is God. He is not of the same ilk as humankind and should not be treated as such. We come dangerously close to blasphemy when we refer to God as a friend, a buddy, or a coworker. Yes, God accompanies us, but never for a moment forget that he is a holy God.

Isaiah understood the holiness of God. Over thirty times this Old Testament prophet called God the "Holy One of Israel." In one of the most powerful scenes in Scripture, Isaiah describes his reaction to the holiness of God. The prophet, transported to a high and exalted state, was in the presence of God. The holy creatures veiled their faces before the infinitely greater holiness of God. Isaiah heard them exclaim, "Holy, holy, holy is the LORD Almighty; the whole earth is full of his glory" (Isa. 6:3). Isaiah knew he was in a hallowed presence.

In this encounter with a holy God, we find another reason that keeps many from a life of morality. We fail to realize the projection of God's holiness onto our character. A direct relationship exists between the degree of one's sense of God's holiness and the quality of one's character. Isaiah experienced this sense to a devastating degree. In viewing the holiness of God he saw himself as he really was—sinful and unclean. If God is the epitome of moral excellence, humankind is the epitome of moral depravity. Isaiah cried, "Woe to me! . . . I am ruined! For I am a man of unclean lips, and I live among a people of unclean lips, and my eyes have seen the King, the LORD Almighty" (v. 5).

When we enter the presence of God, our corruption, our sinfulness, and our depravity are revealed. Even "all our righteous acts are like filthy rags" (Isa. 64:6). Only in the presence of God can we view sin as it really is—an evil against God's character. W. S. Plumer was right in asserting that "we never see sin aright until we see it as against God."[2]

Our desire for a moral life, furthermore, is hindered when all sin is not taken seriously. Our society winks at what we used to weep about. We have reclothed immorality and made it acceptable. If we are not careful we, as believers in Jesus Christ, begin to categorize sin on a continuum: not too bad . . . bad . . . really bad . . . awfully bad. We rate sin in levels—from that which is intolerable to that which is at times acceptable. But with God sin is sin. There are no levels. When we enter the presence of God, it is not the degree of the wrong but the majesty of God that overwhelms us. Consequently, the holiness of God teaches us that sin must be dealt with—radically, seriously, painfully, and constantly. Isaiah felt this pain. "Then one of the seraphs flew to me with a live coal in his hand, which he had taken with tongs from the altar. With it he touched my mouth and said, 'See, this has touched your lips; your guilt is taken away and your sin atoned for'" (6:6–7).

Also, in failing to take sin seriously, our usefulness to God is thwarted. In the development of distinctive character, God fills us with himself. Since God is holy, the structures that house godly character—our lives—must be clean. On a hot day, we would never quench our thirst with ice-cold lemonade poured into a dirty germ-infested glass. We would find a clean glass. In like manner, God will only pour his holy character into a pure and moral person.

It was only after Isaiah was cleansed that he was useful for service. He had been dirty and broken, but God cleansed him and made him whole. Not until his sin was revealed did Isaiah understand the need for cleansing. Not until Isaiah realized his utter sinfulness did God see the prophet as a useful candidate for service. Isaiah could only make an impact on his world when he became pure and spotless. "Then I heard the voice of the Lord saying, 'Whom shall I send? And who will go for us?' And I said, 'Here am I. Send me!' He said, 'Go and tell this people . . .'" (Isa. 6:8–9).

The apostle Paul in his letter to young Timothy also expressed the need for purity in order to serve. "Nevertheless, God's solid foundation stands firm, sealed with this inscription: 'The Lord knows those who are his,' and, 'Everyone who confesses the name of the Lord must turn away from wickedness.' In a large house there are articles not only of gold and silver, but also of wood and clay; some are for noble purposes and some for ignoble. If a man cleanses himself from the latter, he will be an instrument for noble purposes, made holy, useful to the Master and prepared to do any good work" (2 Tim. 2:19–21).

Deep in the heart of every true believer of Christ is the desire to be useful to the Master, to be a vessel for noble purposes,— prepared for every good work. I desire to be such a vessel, pure and holy, so God can fill me with his nature. But I understand, as the following poem describes, that sin must be dealt with, and I must be cleansed and purified.

> The Master was searching for a vessel to use,
> On the shelf there were many—which one would he
>     choose?
> "Take me!" cried the gold one, so shiny and bright,
> "I'm of great value, and I do things just right.
> My beauty and luster would outshine the rest,
> And for someone like you, Master, I would be best."
>
> The Master passed on with no word at all,
> He looked at a silver urn, narrow and tall.

"I'll serve you, dear Master; I'll pour out your wine,
And be at your table whenever you dine.
My lines are so graceful, and my carvings so true,
And silver would always compliment you."

Unheeding, the Master passed on to the brass,
It was wide-mouthed and shallow and polished like glass.
"Here! Here!" cried that vessel, "I know I will do.
Place me on your table for all men to view."

"Look at me!" cried the goblet of crystal so clear,
"My transparency shows my contents so dear.
Though fragile am I, I will serve you with pride,
And I'm sure I'd be happy in your house to abide."

The Master came next to a vessel of wood,
Polished and carved, it solidly stood.
"You may use me, dear Master," the wooden bowl said.
"But I'd rather you use me for fruit—please, no bread."

Then the Master looked down and saw a vessel of clay,
Empty and broken, it helplessly lay.
No hope had this vessel that the Master might choose
To cleanse and make whole, to fill and to use.
"Ah! This is the vessel I'd been hoping to find,
I will clean it and mend it and make it all mine.

"I need not the vessel with pride of itself,
Nor the one so narrow who sits on the shelf,
Not the one who is big-mouthed and shallow and loud,
Nor the one who displays its contents so proud.
Not that one who thinks he can do all things just right,
But this plain, earthen vessel filled with my power and
        might."

Then gently he lifted the vessel of clay,
Mended and cleansed it and filled it that day.
He spoke to it kindly, "There's work you must do,
You pour out to others, and I'll pour into you."[3]
—Author Unknown

## Guidelines for Living a Moral Life

Once we realize our dire need for God's great work in our lives, we begin to rely on his strength and power. Then, and only then, are we in a position to allow God's good graces to begin fashioning something akin to goodness out of our lives. This fashioning is not easy, nor is it painless. And it doesn't happen overnight. But it is fruitful. Several activities occur in the process of attaining goodness.

### *Confession*

The first activity is that of confession. Because sin is the obstacle to a moral life, it must be dealt with quickly and effectively. Confession is facing sin and admitting our wrong before a holy and righteous God. "If we confess our sins, he is faithful and just and will forgive us our sins and purify us from all unrighteousness" (1 John 1:9). Confession is to agree with God. He knows our transgressions against his holy character. All we can say is, "Yes, Lord, I blew it again. Please forgive me."

Confession is perpetual and arduous. I remember the first time my daddy had me pick up rocks in an open field so he could plant a garden. *This won't be difficult,* I thought. I noticed several large boulders that needed to be rolled off to the side of the field. With the help of my twin brother, the larger rocks were quickly moved away. But when I turned around I discovered a miracle, or rather a curse. Once the large boulders were removed, several dozen stones the size of baseballs percolated to the top.

Now the real work began as I tossed rocks into a wheelbarrow. After hundreds of bends and stoops the field was cleared. But, again, I had made a false assumption. Once the boulders and rocks were removed, hundreds of smaller stones were revealed. *This rock-clearing task will never end,* I thought.

Confessing sin is like that. The larger, more blatant sins are easy to detect. But the dozens of smaller sins, lying just below the surface of our lives, require the real work—the ongoing clearing through confession.

In performing the work of confession, however, we fail to deal with blind spots—weaknesses and deeply entrenched habits that can sabotage our best intentions to attain purity. Moral sickness is rarely the result of a catastrophic malignancy; almost always it is the result of myriad little ills. When we fail to detect those little ills, eventually we completely forget our weaknesses and shortcomings. Then we begin to rename these wrongs. Prejudice becomes conviction, stealing is simply adjusting the expense account, or a hot temper is standing firm on principles. We all are guilty of these little deceptions every time we fail to face our sin by confessing it. Consequently, ugly and dirty immoral behavior grows like a cancer until it destroys a beautiful life.

An alternative, however, exists. The confession of sin leads to cleansing. The divine Physician in his infinite and merciful way takes his heavenly scalpel and cuts away at the malignant cancer until we are whole and holy. When we are cleansed, God can begin to fill us, use us, and imprint his character upon us.

## Transformation

Once we do our work of confession, God is able to begin his work of transformation—the second activity. The Christian life involves constant change. When we came to faith in Christ, we changed our direction. Theologians refer to it as *justification.* As we walk with Christ we are changed into his likeness—

*sanctification.* And one day we will step into heaven and ultimately be changed—*glorification.*

Consider sanctification. Transformation is the continual casting off of the old self and putting on of the new self. As the apostle Paul said, "You were taught, with regard to your former way of life, to put off your old self, which is being corrupted by its deceitful desires . . . and to put on the new self, created to be like God in true righteousness and holiness" (Eph. 4:22, 24). God can do his transforming work when we confess and, subsequently, turn away from sin.

A miraculous change occurs when a caterpillar is transformed into a monarch butterfly. The evidence of the miracle is in seeing the change. In like manner, those who are transformed by Christ experience a change in their thoughts and attitudes, which leads to a change in behavior. As Paul reminded the Roman church, "Do not conform any longer to the pattern of this world, but be transformed by the renewing of your mind" (Rom. 12:2). To be *transformed* means to be changed within. According to John Murray, "The term used here implies that we are to be constantly in the process of being metamorphosed by renewal of that which is the seat of thought and understanding."[4] We are changed on the outside because of what the Holy Spirit is doing on the inside. Because of the work of the Holy Spirit we are continually in the process of being changed into the likeness of Jesus.

At the center of these changes is a renewal of values and desires. We gain a new perspective on life. As one old-timer has said, "A Christian can do anything he wants to, because God changes his want to's." We now see life through God's eyes. Some practices that we once thought acceptable are no longer tolerable. The moral life is lived in conformity to the commands and desires of Holy Scriptures.

We cannot take full responsibility for moral goodness. Our moral life, like our immortal life, is dependent on God. Only God can produce earthly and eternal changes.

## Repentance

As we continue to do our work of confession and God increasingly does his work of transformation, we note something wondrous. Repentance—the third activity—takes on new meaning. Often we think of repentance as what occurs at the point of salvation. But repentance is a constant activity throughout a believer's walk toward moral excellence. Repentance is more than feeling sorry or even acknowledging sin. Repentance is having the mind of God concerning sin. Sin is serious business to God. It should be to us. God is a holy God who abhors the presence of sin. We should view our sin in the same manner.

Repentance prods us to walk away from sin. The apostle Paul instructed his readers to "flee from sexual immorality" (1 Cor. 6:18), "flee from idolatry" (10:14), flee from the love of money (1 Tim. 6:10–11), and "flee the evil desires of youth" (2 Tim. 2:22). Fleeing sin is repentance in action. The Bible instructs us to stand against Satan (in the name of Jesus), but to run away from sin. We would do well to employ those two distinct strategies at the appropriate times.

Steve came to Christ as a senior in high school. He earnestly wanted to please Christ and walk in a manner that would glorify his name. Steve was bright and handsome. He had been a standout athlete in high school and went to college on a football scholarship. His first weekend home from college he stopped by my office. "You wouldn't have believed it, Rick," he started. "I wasn't at college more than three hours when several of the junior and senior football players invited me to their apartment. All the vices I left behind before I came to Christ were present— beer, willing girls, and daring guys. I wanted to be friends with these fellow athletes, but I knew if I didn't leave I would stumble and fall into a trap. I walked out the door almost as soon as I walked through it. Did I do right?"

"You bet," I affirmed.

We always do right when we walk away from sin and its alluring charm. Even if it means losing friends or recognition, pleasing God by living a holy life is always best.

In practical terms, we need to know ourselves well enough to recognize those situations that induce sin. There are certain television channels and Internet sites we have no business viewing. There are certain people whom, because of their negative influences, we should avoid. There are settings too tempting, touches too personal, and liberties too captivating for us to handle. We are fools to play around with them. We must run from them as fast as we can.

## Courage

Remember that pleasing God by living a holy life is not always easy or popular. We're in a war, and maintaining holiness is a series of constant battles. That is where the fourth activity—courage—enters the picture. The apostle Paul displayed courage when he wrote to the church at Thessalonica, "Yet God gave us the courage to boldly repeat the same message to you, even though we were surrounded by enemies" (1 Thess. 2:2 LB). Courage is the ability to do what is right even when we don't have to. It is living out our convictions and commitments as we say *no* to those things that would bring us down.

The opposite of courage is not cowardice but conformity. The desire of the world is conformity, and the "pack" mentality pervades. "Be one of the boys," "Go along with the crowd," "Come on, everyone is doing it" are common watchwords of the world's philosophy.

Henry David Thoreau, a rugged individualist of the nineteenth century, once went to jail rather than pay his poll tax to a state that supported slavery. During this period he wrote his world-famous essay entitled "Civil Disobedience."

Thoreau's good friend, Ralph Waldo Emerson, came to visit

him in jail. Peering through the bars Emerson asked, "Why are you here?"

Thoreau replied, "Why are you not here?"[5]

In another setting Thoreau commented, "If a man does not keep pace with his companions perhaps it is because he hears a different drummer. Let him step to the music which he hears, however measured or far away."[6] To win the battle for morality one must have the courage to be different, even to be regarded as peculiar, because one is marching to the drumbeat of a different Drummer.

Courage is standing for what is right. Let's be honest, in every instance it's not possible to walk away from tempting situations. At those moments we must take a stand. We must show the crowd—the world—who we are and whom we serve.

Martin Luther demonstrated courage by nailing his Ninety-five Theses to the door of the Wittenberg Chapel. Exposing the heresy and hypocrisy of the Roman Catholic Church in a speech at the Diet of Worms, he stated, "Here I stand. I can do no other. God help me. Amen."[7]

At a national sales convention a heralded speaker delivered a motivational talk. His speech was punctuated with profanity and with God's name used in vain. Finally, a Christian salesman in the audience could stand it no longer. He rose from his seat, stood on his chair, and shouted, "Please leave God out of it." With that he sat down. The speaker cleaned up the remainder of his speech. Following the address a longer line of people waited to shake the Christian's hand than to shake the hand of the motivational speaker. Courage was demonstrated and subsequently rewarded.

## Confidence

Christians need not be defensive as they face an immoral world. But they do need confidence—the fifth activity. Consider this instruction tucked away in the New Testament: "Herod feared John and protected him, knowing him to be a righteous and holy man" (Mark 6:20). When we are righteous and holy as John was, the world around us develops a fear—or better, a respect—for us as we identify with Christ. We need never feel awkward or apologetic when we deviate from the world's standard. Others will be more afraid of us than we are afraid of social rejection. Confidence breeds energy. The energy grows into vigor for a moral life.

Confident living is directly linked to being moral—free from impurity and deception. There's no security like being free from blame. When we are living morally we can smile at life. We can take its pressures and enjoy its pleasures.

In a California courtroom, four men were convicted of financial fraud and sentenced to seven-and-a-half years in federal prison. Five men were originally investigated, but the fifth, Mark Jacobs, was not arrested and charged. Jacobs had been invited by the other four, his good friends from a weekly Bible study, to join the financial scheme. They had assured him that their plan was totally legal. Yet something inside him said it wasn't right. While it was hard to say no to good friends, he chose to go with his conscience and told them he wouldn't participate.

The lawyers for the four convicted men pleaded with the judge that their clients had simply exercised poor judgment. They were good men who loved their wives and kids, gave to charities, and were active in their churches. Their crime involved a "gray" area, crossing a line that wasn't clear.

The judge disagreed. "It is not hard to determine where the line is," he said. "The guy who drew the line is Mark Jacobs. He knew what was right and what was wrong, and he didn't hesitate. Hopefully, now we will have fewer people who are willing to walk up to the line and dabble with going over the line. We will have people like Mr. Jacobs who wouldn't touch this thing with a ten-foot pole."

Mark Jacobs had the courage to do what was right. He had the courage to walk away. May his tribe increase.

## Fellowship

Probably one of the best assets for living a moral life is the companionship of growing Christians—fellowship, the final activity. Committed believers give us the strength to stand strong day after day. One person can often be overrun, but by standing with others against sin we become as a fortified wall, impossible for the enemy to scale or break down. Resisting evil becomes a team effort. "Two are better than one, because they have a good return for their work: If one falls down, his friend can help him up. But pity the man who falls and has no one to help him up!" (Eccl. 4:9–10). When we walk with the strong we grow strong.

The selection of our companions and friends becomes an important element in our battle against temptation and for moral purity. The apostle Paul reminded us, "Do not be misled: 'Bad company corrupts good character'" (1 Cor. 15:33). As wrong friends can steer us toward evil, godly companions can help us stay on the right path. Paul exhorted Timothy to "flee the evil desires of youth, and pursue righteousness, faith, love and peace, along with those who call on the Lord out of a pure heart" (2 Tim. 2:22). *Those* refers to honest friends, fellow believers, and faithful companions. A team effort is required for living morally in an immoral world.

Migrating geese provide an excellent example of teamwork. When the geese fly south toward the rice fields of the American Gulf Coast, they always fly in a *V* formation. Two scientists employed a wind tunnel to determine why the birds continually use this formation. Each goose, by flapping its wings, creates lift for the bird that follows. Consequently, the flock gains 71 percent greater flying range as a team than when a goose flies alone. We, too, when flying together as a team and experiencing the nurture and discipline of fellow believers, will reach new heights in the quest for goodness.

## Being Light in the Dark

Moral behavior in an immoral world is attainable. One can rise above the crowd and live with distinction. Ken proved that. So did Steve. So did Mark Jacobs. And so can you. A distinctive, moral character is within reach and can be displayed every day, even in a world that counters it and does not expect it.

Once when the Cleveland Symphony Orchestra was performing "The Magic Flute" by Mozart, an electrical storm caused the lights to go out. Undaunted by the difficulties, the members of the orchestra knew the music so well that they completed the performance in the dark. At the end of the performance, the audience burst into thunderous applause, and a stagehand illuminated the orchestra and conductor with a flashlight so that they could take their bows.

It is much the same in the spiritual realm. If we know the Master, we can play his music even in the dark. We can exhibit a moral life in an immoral world. We can live a life of distinction.

*Chapter 4*

# FOSTERING A DYNAMIC RELATIONSHIP WITH GOD

... and to goodness, knowledge ...

—2 Peter 1:5

Integrity without knowledge is weak and useless, and knowledge without integrity is dangerous and dreadful.[1]

—Samuel Johnson

When asked what he knew about God, George Beverly Shea, soloist for the Billy Graham crusades, replied, "Not much, but — what I do know has changed my life!"

Of all the subjects we can study, only one can make sense out of life. We can learn how to become wealthy, or we can amass knowledge about increasing physical strength, we can study time management to efficiently use our time, we can take seminars and attend graduate schools to enhance our vocational expertise, we can learn the intricacies of our hobbies. But only the knowledge of God will make an eternal difference. Over a century ago a twenty-year-old preacher, Charles Spurgeon, entered the pulpit of New Park Street Chapel, Southwark, England. He said, "The highest science, the loftiest speculation, the mightiest philosophy, which can ever engage the attention of a child of God, is the name, the nature, the person, the work, the doings, and the existence of the great God whom he calls his Father."[2]

Do you want to rise above the crowd? Do you want to live a distinctive life? Do you want to find true success? Do you want to discover the truth about yourself? Do you want to gain wisdom for every day? Do you want to discover guidance and direction for the future? Do you want to decide what is right and honorable in daily circumstances? Do you want to understand the practical effects of all decisions? Then you must take your eyes off yourself and focus them on the Lord. You must begin the life-long pursuit of knowing God. In his book, *Knowing God*, J. I. Packer warned, "Disregard the study of God, and you sentence yourself to stumble and blunder through life blindfolded, as it were, with no sense of direction and no understanding of what surrounds you. This way you can waste your life and lose your soul."[3] Life consists not in the pursuit of material success but in the quest for spiritual growth. Our entire earthly existence is but a transitional stage in the movement to something higher. And that something higher is a life-changing, character-transforming relationship with the God of the universe.

Moral excellence cleans the life, making it pure and holy. But as a structure, that life would remain empty if nothing filled it. In the life of distinctive character, the knowledge of God fills the newly purified life. Peter wrote, "Make every effort to add to your faith goodness; and to goodness, knowledge" (2 Peter 1:5). The quest to build a distinctive character requires a compulsion to know God.

## Knowing God

Can a person know God? Is it possible that finite humans can know an infinite being? The answer is yes, on three levels.

## *Revelation: Knowing of God*

Theologians call knowledge *of* God revelation. "For all that may be known of God by men lies plain before their eyes; indeed God himself has disclosed it to them" (Rom. 1:19 NEB). All people know of God. He has given us a general revelation of himself in the handiwork of the heavens: "The heavens declare the glory of God; the skies proclaim the work of his hands" (Ps. 19:1).

When you look into the heavens on a clear night, you know that the stars didn't just tumble into space. The rising and the lowering of the tide; the sprouting of a plant from a seed dropped into the ground; the climates, the breezes, the weather, the wind currents that sweep across the earth—those things don't "just happen."

My breath has quickened at the sight of the rugged Santa Lucia Mountain Range where it descends into the blue Pacific waters. I have gazed at the towering redwoods in California, the majestic Swiss Alps, and sunsets from the beaches of Maui. I have stood speechless at the rim of the Grand Canyon. I have been amazed by the geysers and hot springs of Yellowstone. For me, it would take more faith to believe that these wonders happened by chance than to believe that Earth and the universe were created by a Master Designer, whose power and greatness are beyond human understanding.

The creation of the universe is obviously from the hand of the living God. One has to train oneself *not* to think that way. In fact, we have to teach our children not to believe in God. The natural heart of a child believes that someone outside him- or herself arranged the things of this world and keeps them in motion.

## *Religion: Knowing About God*

Knowing *about* God is the function of religion. Religion has been described in many ways—the moral instinct that acknowledges a

Supreme Being upon whom man is dependent and to whom he is responsible; following a set pattern of dos and don'ts; an outward expression with no inward authenticity; human effort to reach God. Anselm, the famous eleventh-century Italian theologian, stated that the idea of God in the mind is proof that God exists. Pascal, the seventeenth-century French physicist and philosopher, spoke about the God-shaped vacuum in everyday life that only God can fill. Understand, though, that religion at its best only knows God in principle without knowing him in person.

Billy Graham is a hero of mine. He epitomizes the Christian statesman. He is known for preaching the gospel to millions of people throughout the world while keeping intact his high moral fiber, ethical integrity, and sincere humility. I know that he was born in North Carolina, came to faith in Christ when the evangelist Mordecai Ham was preaching, went to Bible College in Florida, and later transferred and graduated from Wheaton College, outside of Chicago. He was one of the early leaders in the Youth for Christ movement and was the president of Northwestern College in Minneapolis. His first big crusade was in Los Angeles in 1948, and his media popularity was helped by William Randolph Hearst, who directed his publications to "push Graham." Today the Billy Graham Evangelistic Organization is a multimillion-dollar operation that not only provides crusade evangelism throughout the world, but also has a film production company and a book publishing firm, plus numerous other ministries. I know all of that and more about Billy Graham, but I don't know him—I have never met him.

Do you see the difference? One can possess a catalog of facts about the Supreme Being without having a personal relationship with him.

John Wesley, the founder of the Methodist church, went to Oxford Seminary for five years. He then served for ten years as a minister of the Church of England. Near the end of this decade of ministry, in 1735, he became a missionary from England to

Georgia. Up until this time his ministry had been a failure, though he would have been described as devoutly religious. He awoke at 4:00 A.M. to pray for two hours. He then read his Bible for an hour before going to the jails, prisons, and hospitals to minister to all types of people. He taught, and prayed, and served others until late at night. He worked this schedule for years.

On his way back from America, the ship on which he was a passenger encountered a storm. The ship was about to sink, and Wesley was in terror for his life. He had no assurance of what would happen to him when he died. Despite all of his efforts to be good, death now held only fear—a big, black question mark.

On the other side of the ship a group of men were singing hymns. He asked them, "How can you sing this very night you are going to die?"

They replied, "If this ship goes down we will go up to be with the Lord."

Wesley went away shaking his head thinking, *How can they know that? What more have they done than I have done?* Then he thought, *I came to convert the heathen, but who shall convert me?*

In the providence of God, the ship did not sink, and Wesley returned to England. In London he found his way to a small chapel on Aldersgate Street. He heard a sermon that described faith as a personal relationship with Jesus Christ.

Wesley suddenly realized that he had been on the wrong road all his life. He, like a lot of us, had been religious—he knew about God, but he had not had a personal encounter with God. His was head knowledge of God but not heart knowledge. He knew facts about God but he did not have faith in God.

Saul of Tarsus was also religious.

> If anyone else thinks he has reasons to put confidence in
> the flesh, I have more: circumcised on the eighth day, of
> the people of Israel, of the tribe of Benjamin, a Hebrew
> of Hebrews; in regard to the law, a Pharisee; as for zeal,

persecuting the church; as for legalistic righteousness, faultless. But whatever was to my profit I now consider loss for the sake of Christ. (Phil. 3:4–7)

How does Paul view his religious credentials? As "loss." That is a polite way of saying they are like garbage, rubbish, or dung. He is not implying that his works (or my or your religious efforts) are worthless or meaningless, but they do not satisfy his hunger for God. They might help him know about God, but they do not help him know God.

## Relationship: Knowing God Personally

John Naisbitt, author of *Megatrends*, wrote about the current status of our culture: "We are drowning in information and starved for knowledge."[4] Naisbitt likely did not realize that his statement had relevance to one's search for God. Our quest for a distinctive character is far more than merely knowing of God or knowing about God. We need to move from revelation, through religion, to a relationship—knowing God personally.

Knowing God personally is where one encounters God and experiences God through a personal relationship. Paul was consumed with a desire to know God. It was the most important pursuit in his life. "I consider everything a loss compared to the surpassing greatness of knowing Christ Jesus my Lord" (Phil. 3:8). Paul describes his personal relationship with God by employing an interesting word—*know. Know* is a relational word that indicates personal knowledge, not simply intellectual knowledge.

In biblical times *know* was an intimate word. Often, it was used to express the highest form of intimacy—sexual intercourse. Biblical writers were modest by today's standards. They wrote, "Adam knew Eve" (Gen. 4:1 KJV), or "I have two daughters which have not known man" (Gen. 19:8 KJV). Rather than describe the physical sexual act, the biblical writers conveyed it through the word *know.*

The word *know* refers to knowledge gained by the senses, not knowledge acquired purely by rational thought. *Knowing* speaks of an intimate relationship in which, as ministers often say at a wedding ceremony, the two have become one. Picture two sheets of paper glued together in such a fashion that they become like one piece of paper. The sheets are virtually impossible to separate, and any attempt to pull the sheets apart will tear both papers. This illustrates intimacy at its highest form. When one is hurt, the other suffers. When one is attacked, the other adheres even tighter.

*Know,* used in reference to the knowledge of God, conveys the idea of a dynamic, intimate relationship between God—who is sovereign—and us, his beloved. God has made himself known through his creation, his acts, and his Son. Now we can know him through an intimate experience.

Intimacy with God is more than acknowledging his revelation through creation, even though one has to stand in awe of his work. Intimacy with God is more than accumulating facts, even though it involves the gaining of facts while humbling and expanding the mind. Intimacy is more than believing in him; it requires trusting him. Intimacy with God is acquired through a day-to-day relationship based on a personal experience of him. The growth of the relationship requires a lifetime commitment to the development and success of this intimacy. Intimacy with God demands patience and endurance. The end result is a life that is changed, distinguished, reflecting the character and nature of Jesus Christ.

Many years ago, a great actor and dramatist traveled throughout America drawing enormous crowds, giving readings from great writers such as Shakespeare. He always ended his performance with a reading from the Bible. Usually it was the Twenty-third Psalm. On one particular occasion he recited the Shepherd's Psalm with great power, raising and lowering the intensity of his delivery to get the maximum effect.

The crowd was spellbound.

When he finished, the audience applauded. He bowed, very thrilled with the reception. Over to the right side of the auditorium an older gentleman rose very slowly. Most of the audience recognized the older gentleman. He was a retired preacher. He walked onto the stage, stood in front of the crowd, turned to the actor, and asked, "Sir, how beautiful that was; would you let me recite the Twenty-third Psalm, too?"

The actor, somewhat taken aback, reluctantly said, "Of course."

The preacher's voice wasn't as strong as it once was, and he wasn't learned in the nuances of drama. "The Lord is my shepherd," he began. "I shall not want . . ." He continued sharing the words of David's beautiful Psalm and came to the close: "Surely goodness and mercy shall follow me all the days of my life and I will dwell in the house of the Lord forever."

There wasn't a sound. Nobody moved. Then a woman wiped the tears away. A man nearby pulled out his handkerchief. No one applauded, but it was obvious that the entire audience was deeply moved. The great dramatist could contain himself no longer. He addressed the retired minister, "Sir, when I gave the Twenty-third Psalm there was great applause. But when you recited it without the proper intonation and inflection, people cried. I feel like crying myself. What's the difference?"

The old pastor said, "Well, sir, you spoke better than I. But the difference, I suppose, is that you know the Psalm but I know the Shepherd. I know him as the Lord of my life. He has walked with me in the deep waters of my sorrows. He's been with me on the mountaintops of my joys. He has been with me in sickness and health. And now as I take my last steps I'll soon be with him in glory. You see he's everything to me. He's my Shepherd. I know the Shepherd."[5]

Nothing can compare with knowing God intimately and personally. Knowing God is to know him as a friend knows a friend or as a lover knows a lover.

Do you want to know God in this way?

# The Process of Knowing God Intimately

God is actually alive. I think we sometimes forget that. And it is his business to open our eyes to him so that we can know him. God unfolds himself like an opening rose. The fragrance of his sweetness permeates our souls. The softness of his touch envelops our beings. The radiance of his beauty glows triumphantly through us. It is true that we will never know God perfectly, but we can certainly know him better—much, much better.

God is a person, not simply a power. We get to know him like we would know another person. And that—as with all good relationships—takes time. The way to improve the quality of time with God is through increasing the quantity of time with God. Just as a lasting friendship or a strong marriage requires frequent conversations and a variety of shared experiences over months and years, so does our relationship with our heavenly Father. As wonderful as new friendships may be, the best friendships are those that have been developed over a lifetime. Those who have become more intimately acquainted with God share some characteristics in common with one another.

## Brokenness

First, knowing God begins with brokenness—our will must be broken to his will. As painful and humiliating as it may seem, brokenness is the only position from which to know God. God said through the prophet Isaiah, "This is the one I esteem: he who is humble and contrite in spirit, and trembles at my word" (Isa. 66:2). The apostle Paul expressed that humility and contrition. "I have been crucified with Christ and I no longer live, but Christ lives in me" (Gal. 2:20).

Christ can neither live fully in believers nor fruitfully reveal himself through them until the proud self is broken. The unyielding self that abhors compromise and surrender, the self that justifies and desires its own way must humbly bow before God, admit it is wrong, give up its own way to Christ, and surrender its rights in order that Christ might have all and be all. A daily humbling of rights and interests before the all-wise and all-loving God of the universe must occur.

You've probably heard it said that God helps those who help themselves. That's inaccurate. The truth is that God helps those who realize their need for help. Until we recognize our need for God and his role in our lives, he can't assist us.

Jesus, broken on the cross, serves as the compelling motive for our brokenness. Jesus, as God, did not count equality with God as a prize to be grasped, but gave it up for us. He took upon himself the form of a servant. He had no rights, men reviled him. He was beaten, bruised, and broken on behalf of us all.

Anne Ortlund, in her book *Up with Worship*, expressed the beauty of brokenness by expounding on the occasion when Mary broke a vase of perfume for Jesus.

> A while back, Ray [Anne's husband] preached on Mark 14:3. "Here comes Mary, . . . with her alabaster vase of nard to the dinner where Jesus was. She broke the bottle and poured it on him."
>
> An alabaster vase—milky white, veined, smooth, precious.
>
> And pure nard inside! Gone forever. According to John 12:3, the whole house became filled with the fragrance. Some story.

---

> Christians file into church on a Sunday morning. One by one by one they march in—like separate alabaster vases.
>
> Contained.
>
> Self-sufficient.

Encased.

Individually complete.

Contents undisclosed.

No perfume emitting at all.

Their vases aren't bad looking. In fact, some of them are the Beautiful People, and they become Vase-Conscious: conscious of their own vase and of one another's. They're aware of clothes, of personalities, of position in this world—of exteriors.

So before and after church (maybe during) they're apt to talk Vase talk.

---

Mary broke her vase.

Broke it?! How shocking. How controversial. Was everybody doing it? Was it a vase-breaking party? No, she just did it all by herself. What happened then? The obvious: all the contents were forever released. She could never hug her precious nard to herself again.

---

Many bodies who file into church, no doubt, do so because they have Jesus inside of them. Jesus!—precious, exciting, life giving. But most of them keep Him shut up, contained, enclosed all their lives. And the air is full of *nothing.* They come to church and sit—these long rows of cold, beautiful, alabaster vases! Then the cold, beautiful, alabaster vases get up and march out again, silently— or maybe talking their cold alabaster talk—to repeat the ritual week after week, year after year.

Unless they just get too bored and quit.

The need for Christians everywhere (nobody is exempt)

is to be broken. The vase has to be smashed! Christians have to let the life out! It will fill the room with sweetness. And the congregation will all be broken shards, mingling together for the first time.

Of course it's awkward and scary to be broken! Of course it's easier to keep up that cold alabaster front.

It was costly for Mary too.[6]

Being broken before God is not much different than a piano student submitting to the authority of her teacher in order to advance her skills, or a tennis player humbling himself before a coach in order to play competitively, or a scholar who is open to new discoveries and ideas in order to learn more about her particular field of study.

Being broken is not a once-and-for-all event. It is a continuous act of surrendering self and dying to the world for Jesus' sake. Knowing God requires the continuous yielding of one's choices to God's direction. Amazingly, the reward of brokenness is that as we offer ourselves to God in humility and contrition he gives himself to us in return. The miracle that allowed the feeding of five thousand people was not only proof of the power of Jesus, but also an illustration of the multiplying result of brokenness. In yielding ourselves to Christ, we don't lose, we gain.

## Openness

Openness is the natural outcome of brokenness. Openness is the vulnerability or transparency of one's life to the point of complete self-disclosure. The quality of openness is necessary in building successful friendships and marriages. It is also essential in developing our relationship with God. Alan Loy McGinnis wrote, "There is no substitute for transparency in drawing out the beloved."[7] Surprise of surprises, when we open ourselves to God, he reveals himself to us.

Jesus demonstrated transparency to his followers throughout his ministry. He expressed to them his concerns, hurts, fears, and needs. Furthermore, Jesus completely opened his life before his heavenly Father. On the night before his crucifixion, Jesus earnestly prayed that God would spare him from the cross. He laid his heart and soul bare before God. He was hurting. He sought another way. The Son of God was transparent. As he had throughout his life on earth, he demonstrated the attitude of openness that is required to know God.

Robert Boyd Munger's poignant essay *My Heart—Christ's Home* describes inviting Christ into one's heart like having a friend come to live in one's home.[8] The heart is a home with many rooms. Christ enters the study, the dining room, the drawing room, the workshop, and the playroom. When Christ moves into the rooms of the heart, changes are made. At times the changes are painful, sometimes embarrassing, and at other times awkward.

On occasion Christ may wait at the door of a new believer's heart and say, "There is a peculiar odor in the house. Something is dead around here. It's upstairs. I'm sure it is in the hall closet." Yes, there in the hall closet are some personal things that the believer did not want Christ to see.

When Christ enters one's life he wants it all. He wants us to lay bare everything in our lives and to be honest with him. He wants us to open all the rooms for his use, and by doing so we gain a paradoxical victory. Allowing Christ to clean the filth from the hall closet allows freedom and joy to invade all of the heart. The new believer realizes that Christ should take over full management of the entire heart and home and life, because when Christ enters he brings his warmth, his joy, and his laughter.

What are you hiding from God? What are your secrets? If we wish to deepen our relationship with God, our fears, our hurts, our hang-ups, our sin, and our needs must be exposed. A friend said, "In gut-wrenching honesty and painstaking candor I bared myself before an all-seeing and all-knowing heavenly Father.

When I completely opened myself to him, he embraced me with his tenderness and gentleness, revealing the secrets of his heart. I will never live life without complete and total vulnerability. It is the only peaceful way to enter the presence of God." My friend is right. Only through openness and honesty will we see and know God.

It seems that various levels of friendship exist. First, the acquaintance level that is based on occasional contacts. Second, the casual level, based on common interests, activities, and concerns. Third, close friendship that is based on mutual goals. Fourth, the intimate level that is based on complete openness and vulnerability. Apply these levels to the knowledge of God. What level are you on? Are you intimate with God? Are there any secret chambers in your heart? Have you opened your heart to the Lord?

## Eagerness

Men and women who pursue and attain graduate and post-graduate degrees are an inspiration to me. These rare individuals hunger and thirst for knowledge. Most of them are not content with merely hanging the coveted diploma on the wall. Instead, they continue to study and research in order to gain new insight into their respective fields of interest.

A similar drive compels believers in their search for God. Jeremiah understood the value of knowing God and the effort it required. In his first letter to the exiles in Babylon, he addressed them as a messenger. "'For I know the plans I have for you,' declares the LORD, 'plans to prosper you and not to harm you, plans to give you hope and a future. Then you will call upon me and come and pray to me, and I will listen to you. You will seek me and find me when you seek me with all your heart. I will be found by you,' declares the LORD" (Jer. 29:11–14). Jeremiah wanted these people to realize that just because they were many miles from home they were not separated from God. God could be found in Babylon as well as Jerusalem.

The word *find* suggests that a believer can gain an intimate, personal relationship with God. Locale is not important but attitude is essential. In all earnestness, then, the believer should endeavor to press into fellowship with God. Notice the repetition of the word *me*. It is used five times, the repetition providing insight into what the believer should seek—his person. We must look for who he is and not what he can do. The people of Israel had been crying for deliverance, but Jeremiah said that it was not enough to cry for deliverance. They must seek the Deliverer.

When his plans are good and gracious, why should we not seek the embrace of his person? When will we learn that we need the Deliverer more than the deliverance? We need the One who blesses more than the blessing, the Giver more than the gifts, the Victor more than the victory, the Guide more than the guidance. When we have God, we have all his resources and assistance. When we seek the benefits, we miss the Benefactor and come up short in our quest for knowing God.

Let it be understood that God will not be used. If we seek God for any reason other than to know him, we are idolaters. As good as our intentions may be, God wants to be sought for who he is, not for what he can give. Consider prayer. Our prayer life reveals our heart. If we petition for what God can do rather than praise him for who he is, we are seeking his hand and not his Person. David's prayer serves as a model: "My heart says of you, 'Seek his face!' Your face, LORD, I will seek" (Ps. 27:8).

Jeremiah adds a further condition for the one earnestly seeking to know God: You must seek him "with all your heart." *All your heart* entails a clean heart. We are wasting our time searching for God if sin controls our lives. *All your heart* involves single-mindedness. The pure and single-minded heart desires God, and him alone.

David declared, "One thing I ask of the LORD, this is what I seek: that I may dwell in the house of the LORD all the days of my life, to gaze upon the beauty of the Lord and to seek him in his temple" (Ps. 27:4). The believer compelled to know God in a deeper and dynamic relationship learns to say no to other people and events that would misdirect him or her in maintaining this priority. Our capacity to say *no* determines our capacity to say *yes* to the important things. Don't let the world distract you from the highest and the best—knowing God.

Are you seeking God with all your heart? *All* is a small word that stands for everything. The tragedy of Christianity is that many haven't sought God with all their beings. If the truth be known, we want part of Christianity—joy, peace, eternal life—but not all—total commitment, absolute surrender, daily discipleship. Entering into a powerful relationship with God demands our hearts, our lives, our all.

The founder of the Salvation Army, William Booth, was asked the secret of his spiritual power. He gave an interesting and illuminating reply: "There was a day in my life when I vowed that God would have everything there was to have of William Booth." Years after his death, his daughter was reminded by a friend of what General Booth had vowed. She said, "You know, the vow on its own wasn't the real secret of father's life. The real secret was that *he kept it.*"[9]

Knowing God mandates the same vow from each believer— whatever the cost, whatever the pain, knowing God is worth every encumbrance.

How much do you want of God? Finding him requires seeking him with everything you possess and everything you are. Anything less is wasted effort. But when all is given, God promises fulfillment. You shall find him. God will reveal and give himself to you. "For the eyes of the Lord range throughout the earth to strengthen those whose hearts are fully committed to him" (2 Chron. 16:9).              *whatever...*

## *Closeness*

God is a person and he is known as a person. Why read and study the Bible? To gain more facts? No. We study the Bible to discover the person of God. Why pray? To petition God as a heavenly slot machine? We pray to communicate with God. Why memorize Scripture? To impress less motivated brothers and sisters? We memorize Scripture to emblazon the truth about God on our hearts. Why submit to discipleship? To awe others by personal discipline? We lead a disciplined life in order to capture the benefits of knowing God. The disciplines of the Christian life are not ends in themselves. They help us to grow in the knowledge of God. And there are no substitutes for these disciplines. They are avenues of communication, leading to a greater closeness with God.

Again, Jesus provides an example and motivation for closeness with the Father. The fact that "Jesus grew . . . in favor with God" (Luke 2:52) demonstrates that even Jesus fostered a growing relationship with his heavenly Father. How? Luke gives us clues to the Son's relationship with his Father.

> When all the people were being baptized, Jesus was baptized too. And as he was praying, heaven was opened and the Holy Spirit descended on him in bodily form like a dove. And a voice came from heaven: "You are my Son, whom I love; with you I am well pleased." (Luke 3:21–22)

> At daybreak Jesus went out to a solitary place. (Luke 4:42)

> But Jesus often withdrew to lonely places and prayed. (Luke 5:16)

> One of those days Jesus went out to a mountainside to pray, and spent the night praying to God. (Luke 6:12)

Jesus knew that a dynamic relationship with God is fostered through time alone with him. If knowing God is important, closeness with him will follow.

As we seek to know the person of God, his character and his life make a deeper impression on us. Closeness with God involves, first of all, listening to his Word. François Fenelon has been quoted, "Be silent, and listen to God. Let your heart be in such a state of preparation [when meditating on Scripture] that his Spirit may impress upon you such virtues as will please him. Let all within you listen to him. This silence of all outward and earthly affection and of human thoughts within us is essential if we are to hear his voice." Second, closeness with God helps to create God's nature and character in us. The words and works of God reveal his being. Making those character traits an integral part of our lives invites a change in us. We begin to reflect God's nature. For example, when God says, "I am holy," and we begin to live distinctive lives, we reflect his holiness. Or when the Bible states, "God is love," and we start loving people as God loves us, we imitate his compassion. Third, as we draw closer to God, we live out daily obedience to his commands. "We know that we have come to know him if we obey his commands" (1 John 2:3). It is not sufficient to simply listen to God and meditate on his word. The person who seeks to grow in his or her knowledge of God acts on what he or she hears.

## The Result of the Relationship

The privilege of knowing God is a "hands on" experience, resulting in the conformity of one's life to the character of God. Sinclair Ferguson remarked, "When people truly know God and are growing in a genuine relationship with him . . . their lives are marked by integrity and reliability. They do not treat dishonesty  of the heart or of the lips indifferently. They are, in a word, holy. . . . If we really knew him, it would show in the character of our lives."[10] This deepening relationship with God results in a character transformation. The more one knows of God the greater one's resemblance to his character and his nature.

An American missionary was teaching a class of Chinese girls in a Sunday school. As she told them about Jesus, she was so anxious to express the truth about him that she grew excited in her description. In the middle of her presentation, a little Chinese girl, about eight years old who was attending Sunday school for the first time, raised her hand.

The missionary asked, "What is it, Darling?"

The little girl said, "I know Jesus."

The teacher said, "No, you don't know Jesus. This is the first time you have been here. You have never heard of him before."

The Chinese girl persisted, "But I know him. He lives on my street."

The missionary did not argue with her, but finished teaching the class. When through, she approached the little girl and said, "Come here, Darling. Who is this Jesus that lives on your street?"

The little Chinese girl told the teacher that on her street lived a man who was kind and loving and gracious like this man Jesus. The missionary discovered that this man was a believer in Jesus Christ. His life was so Christlike that when the teacher talked about Jesus, the little girl thought about that man.

*Chapter 5*

# GAINING CONTROL OF YOUR LIFE

... and to knowledge, self-control . . .

—2 Peter 1:6

Character cannot be developed in ease and quiet. Only through experience of trial and suffering can the soul be strengthened, vision cleared, ambition inspired, and success achieved.[1]

—Helen Keller

Henry Wadsworth Longfellow wrote, "Great is the art of beginning, but greater the art is of ending."[2] Many people experience perpetual frustration, not over starting but over completing. If you are like me, you've started dozens of unfinished projects.

I enjoy refinishing antique furniture. Or, rather, I enjoy the finishing of refinishing. The task itself is far from fun. That's why an oak heirloom dresser sits in my basement with only half of the old paint removed. I've been stripping and sanding it for months. Every time I stroll past, the oak treasure seems to tease, "You haven't finished me." I'll complete the project—one day.

Do you know the feeling?

*Great is the art of beginning, but . . .* The completing of household projects is not all that plagues modern man. We are in a constant struggle to gain control over bad habits. Besetting sins become a ball and chain, impossible to break.

A lack of control is familiar to most of us. We criticize too much. We gossip too much. We overeat. We overspend. We indulge in bad habits, thinking one more time won't hurt. Sometimes we simply don't think at all—we react, ignoring our need for self-control. And where has it gotten us? Three-fourths of Americans live in debt. More than a third of the population is overweight and out of shape. And almost half of all women in America have lived or are living with a man to whom they're not married. Clearly, we're losing the struggle to say *no* to ourselves.

Why can't we get out of debt? Why can't we lose weight? Why can't we get in shape? Why can't we say *no* to adultery? We can't because we lack self-control.

Are the fault lines of self-control cracking open wider and wider exposing your real self? Those same problems and frustrations creep into my life. I often feel like the alcoholic who, when queried if he ever attempted to quit drinking, said, "Oh, quitting is no problem. I've quit a thousand times. It's staying off the bottle that I can't conquer."

In the development of character, believers don't lack knowledge or strength; they most often lack will. If I were to ask the average believer what a mature Christian looks like he or she could describe one. If I were to test a man's knowledge of good or evil he would undoubtedly receive high marks. If a woman were to evaluate a tempting situation she would know how she ought to respond. Knowledge is vitally important, but it is not enough. Something else is needed—the ability to take that knowledge and apply it to our lives. And that takes self-control. Self-control is the measure of rising above the crowd. Without it there is no chance at all to achieve a distinctive character.

The theme of self-control can be found throughout the Bible, but it especially permeates Peter's writings:

> Therefore, prepare your minds for action; be self-controlled; set your hope fully on the grace to be given you when Jesus Christ is revealed. (1 Peter 1:13)

The end of all things is near. Therefore be clear minded and self-controlled so that you can pray. (4:7)

Be self-controlled and alert. Your enemy the devil prowls around like a roaring lion looking for someone to devour. (5:8)

For this very reason, make every effort to add to your faith goodness; and to goodness, knowledge; and to knowledge, self-control. (2 Peter 1:5–6)

Peter knew that self-control is essential to character development. He did not talk about it piously; he practiced it rigorously.

So should we. No race is won without it. No temptation is overcome without it. No mind is sharpened without it. No defeating habit is overcome, no right decision is made without it.

## Staying Within the Boundaries

What does it mean to have self-control? Self-control, according to D. G. Kehl, is "the ability to avoid excess, to stay within reasonable bounds."[3] Throughout Scripture God has outlined the boundaries—or standards—for our behavior. Self-control is that virtue that enables us to stay within God-ordained boundaries.

Do you remember coloring books? I loved to color when I was a child. Still do. At first, my attempts at coloring were simply scribbles of crayon on the paper. But as I matured, I learned that for a beautiful picture I needed to stay within the bold lines. The life of distinctive character works the same way. As we mature in faith, our self-control increases, enabling us to live within God's standards.

When the Scriptures speak of self-control, they paint a picture of someone who is master of himself. He has his appetites and emotions under control in order to do what pleases God rather than himself. But self-control is not necessarily the absence of extravagance or spontaneity. Jesus was pleased when Mary poured expensive perfume on his feet.

Self-control is the fruit, or evidence, of the Holy Spirit's work in us. How does this work? The Spirit will not control us in the sense that he will make us do things, but he will give us the ability to control ourselves. There are many things that threaten to control us—habits, greed, selfishness, pride—but the Spirit enables us to have ourselves under control so that, instead of doing what we feel driven to do, we act with self-control. As the Spirit controls us, we refrain from sin because we know that we should. We refrain from sinful pleasures because the deepest part of us understands where real life is found. When we are controlled by the Spirit we want to honor Christ by walking away from those things that displease him and walking toward those things that glorify him. Self-control is achieved when "I want to" practice restraint rather than "I should." It is a decision that comes from knowing God and wanting to please him. True self-control does not bicker and gripe and badger you with negatives. It is a friend who is at your side, encouraging you with incentives and positive reinforcement. Self-control is self-caring, not self-castigating, therefore it should be cultivated.

Displaying a distinctive character is impossible without self-control. The author of Proverbs wrote, "Like a city whose walls are broken down is a man who lacks self-control" (Prov. 25:28). In ancient times the walls of a city were its principal line of protection against an invading army. Without the walls the city was vulnerable—easy prey for an enemy. Since we are at war with our sinful passions, self-control becomes the believer's wall of defense against the sinful desires that wage war against the soul.[4] Charles Bridges describes a person without self-control: "He yields himself to the first assault of his ungoverned passions, offering no resistance. . . . Having no discipline over himself, temptation becomes the occasion of sin, and hurries him on to fearful lengths that he had not contemplated. . . . Anger tends to murder. Unwatchfulness over lust plunges into adultery."[5]

Once the life is under control, a liberating freedom ensues. The Greek philosopher Epictetus was right when he said, "No man is truly free until he masters himself." It is said that retailer J. C. Penney often asserted, "Only the disciplined are free." Often, freedom is defined as living as one pleases. In reality, freedom is behaving as one should. Self-control liberates by enabling us to perform those activities that are essential and mandatory. Self-control is one of the best friends we can have. It will enable us to become the persons we want to be by developing the discipline to perform the activities we want to do. We should cherish this friend always. It molds and maintains a distinguished life.

Yet self-control exacts a high price. Ignance Paderewski, the famed Polish concert pianist, supposedly was approached by an admiring fan following one of his outstanding performances, "I'd give my life to play like that," said the admirer. The brilliant pianist replied, "I did."

On another occasion, it has been reported, Paderewski was asked by a fellow pianist if he could be ready to play a recital on short notice. The famous musician replied, "I am always ready. I have practiced eight hours daily for forty years." The other pianist said, "I wish I had been born with such determination." Paderewski replied, "We are all born with it. I just used mine."

I am not saying that we could be concert pianists just by exercising enough self-control and discipline. But a distinctive character is well within our grasps if we pay the price—apply our wills and come under God's control.

## Where to Begin

Every aspect of one's life needs control. Controlled lives are happier and fuller lives. So where do we begin?

## Mind—thought

Our character is revealed in the way we think because thoughts eventually lead to action. Jerry Bridges wrote, "Our minds are mental greenhouses where unlawful thoughts, once planted, are nurtured and watered before being transplanted into the real world of unlawful actions. People seldom fall suddenly into gluttony or immorality. These actions are savored in the mind long before they are enjoyed in reality. The thought life, then, is our first line of defense in the battle of self-control."[6]

To live controlled lives, our thoughts must be brought under control. Paul said, "We take captive every thought to make it obedient to Christ" (2 Cor. 10:5). Self-control of thoughts means entertaining in our minds only those thoughts that are acceptable to God. The best guideline for controlling our thoughts was given by Paul: "Finally, brothers, whatever is true, whatever is noble, whatever is right, whatever is pure, whatever is lovely, whatever is admirable—if anything is excellent or praiseworthy—think about such things" (Phil. 4:8).

Solomon also offers sound advice: "Above all else, guard your heart, for it is the wellspring of life" (Prov. 4:23). In ancient thinking, the heart was the central organ that controlled all activities and thus determined the character of living. The heart, therefore, must be guarded closely for it is the pivotal source and dominating factor of life. The doorway to the heart is through the ears and eyes.

Are you guarding your heart? Do you control what magazines and television programs you watch? The psalmist wrote, "I will set no worthless thing before my eyes" (Ps. 101:3 NASB). Are you allowing trash to infiltrate your mind? Do you listen to conversations that plant impure and unrighteous thoughts? "Be self-controlled and alert. Your enemy the devil prowls around like a roaring lion looking for someone to devour" (1 Peter 5:8).

## *Body*

A person with self-control has command over his body. "Each of you should learn to control his own body in a way that is holy and honorable" (1 Thess. 4:4). The apostle Paul wrote, "I urge you, brothers, in view of God's mercy, to offer your bodies as living sacrifices, holy and pleasing to God—this is your spiritual act of worship" (Rom. 12:1). Controlling our bodies is a spiritual act. Elisabeth Elliot, in *Discipline: The Glad Surrender,* wrote, "More spiritual failure is due, I believe, to this cause than to any other: the failure to recognize this living body as having anything to do with worship or holy sacrifice. Failure here is failure everywhere else."[7]

Why is the body so important? The body houses the Holy Spirit, who directs our longings to grow in distinctive character.

Would a body inspection reveal haunting facts concerning self-control? For example, the body needs food, but do we consume junk food and empty calories? Is moderation a term that applies to our intake of food and drink? Are we getting the essential vitamins and minerals in our diet?

The body needs sleep, but do we oversleep? Are we lazy? Or are we overworking and neglecting proper rest? A friend often reminds me, "If you're burning the candle at both ends you're not as bright as you think you are." Rest is not something we do when the job is done. Most of us have vocations where the work is never done. We have to discipline ourselves to take time off. A proverb says it best: "If you don't come apart, you will come apart."

What about sex? God's standard for sexual control is absolute abstinence outside of the marriage relationship. Have we fallen prey to the philosophy that sex is permissible at any time as long as it involves two consenting adults?

Eating, sleeping, sex, and any other physical functions are to be for the glory of God. Understanding that every physical activity is a spiritual act will change the way we live.

## *Time*

Self-control also involves our use of time. "Live life, then, with a due sense of responsibility. . . . Make the best use of your time" (Eph. 5:15–16 PHILLIPS). Time is the "stuff" out of which life is built. Alan Lakein, author of *How to Get Control of Your Time and Your Life,* asserts, "Time is life. It is irreversible and irreplaceable. To waste your time is to waste your life, but to master your time is to master your life and make the most of it."[8] As believers, everything in our lives, including the use of time, comes under the lordship of Christ. The psalmist wrote, "But I trust in you, O LORD; I say, 'You are my God.' My times are in your hands" (Ps. 31:14–15). The psalmist understood that controlling time is simply managing it for the Master.

Godly people never seem to be in a hurry but are always moving toward stated objectives. They never seem to be frayed at the ends but working with a quiet, calm countenance. They don't burn out, nor do they rust out. They are busy, involved, and committed to many worthwhile projects, yet they have time for rest, relaxation, and play.

Are you controlling your time or is a lack of time mastering you? Does your schedule reflect a balance? Do you often feel too busy for prayer, Bible study, meditation, and devotions? Does the mere mention of those disciplines cause you to squirm with guilt? Do you allot adequate time for spouse, family, and friends? Do you study other than what is imperative? Do you exercise consistently? Do you get adequate rest?

The wise man recognizes that his time is limited, and therefore, that each minute is of great value. "Teach us to number our days aright, that we may gain a heart of wisdom" (Ps. 90:12). Time is like money: We don't have enough to buy everything, so we buy only that which is worth buying. We learn to say *no* with authority. We learn to budget our time and make the most of it.

Time is precious and priceless. God takes time very seriously. So should we.

## Gaining Control

Do you feel defeated in any of the areas just mentioned? Does gaining control seem like an unscalable mountain? Don't lose hope. Help is available.

How can we acquire self-control? There is no fast and simple formula, but below are some basic guidelines. Undergirding all these suggestions is the submission of one's life to the leadership of Christ and the utilization of the strength and power that is available to us through him.

## *Know Your Objective*

It is impossible to develop self-control without knowing what you want. If you want to run a marathon, you must know how many miles you need to run per day while training to win the race. If you want to lose weight you must know what size you really want to be. To break a bad habit you must know what good habit you want to develop. To mature as a Christian and develop a distinctive character you must have a clear picture of Christlikeness.

Knowing the objective, then, is the principle of direction. Paul said, "In a race everyone runs but only one person gets first prize. So run your race to win. . . . I run straight to the goal. . . . I fight to win" (1 Cor. 9:24, 26 LB). Paul knew what he wanted. He stated his personal goal in his letter to the church at Rome: "It has always been my ambition to preach the gospel where Christ was not known, so that I would not be building on someone else's foundation" (Rom. 15:20). His was not a selfish ambition but a sacred ambition. He looked to God for direction, and he found it. Now he was running to achieve the God-ordained goal.

Walt Disney knew what he wanted. In the midst of failure, a nervous breakdown, and countless people who said his ideas were too far out, his discipline remained intact. His visionary mind brought us Mickey Mouse, Minnie, Pluto, and Donald. It has inspired us through movies, television, and comics. But his greatest dream was the transformation of worthless Florida swampland near the city of Orlando into an enchanting world of motels, hotels, resorts, restaurants, rides, and exhibits—Disney World. As you know, he died before its completion. An admirer remarked, "Too bad Walt didn't get to see this." An associate of Mr. Disney replied, "Oh, but he did."

Knowing what you want is the starting point of discipline. Solomon wrote, "Where there is no vision, the people are unrestrained" (Prov. 29:18 NASB). The word *unrestrained* denotes the picture of an unbridled horse. It runs wild. People without direction are purposeless. They waste energy on less important things because no self-control is employed. Priorities are misplaced because there are no absolutes for which to aim.

## Choose What Is Best

Learn to say *no* to the lesser things in order to say *yes* to the greater things. "To win the contest you must deny yourselves many things that would keep you from doing your best" (1 Cor. 9:25 LB). Self-control is a matter of choice.

Character cannot be legislated nor forced upon someone. It does not come to fruition because someone else requires or commands it of us. Character grows out of knowing what is right and then acting upon it. Self-control is the result of consistently making the right choices. Just as Joshua chose whom he would serve (Josh. 24:15), we must choose whom we will serve, and what we will be, and how we will live.

The development of self-control, therefore, requires the principle of decision. Choosing what is right often requires saying *no* to people and activities. Thus, when we say *yes* to the desire of godly character, we will have to say *no* to many other pursuits. When we learn to say *no*, then we can say *yes* to what matters most.

One of the hallmarks of maturity is this ability to say *no*. I've  worked with young people for many years, and they often ask, "When am I old enough to date?" I respond by saying, "Many factors exist and I'm not trying to boil those down into one simplistic answer, but it seems to me that one factor ventures to the forefront: You are old enough to date when you can say *No!* in any given situation." In truth, some people are never "old" enough.

The ancient, Chinese philosopher Mencius said, "Men must be decided on what they will not do, and then they are able to act with vigor in what they ought to do."[9]

An author was told early in his career, "You'll have to decide whether you are going to be a great writer or a great diner-outer. You can't be both." The late nights out came to an abrupt halt. In order to say *yes* to certain desires you have to say *no* to many others. Self-control extracts a high price. Every goal costs. A price is always paid. Often, the cost is saying *no*.

## Be Intentional

Choosing what is best is an intentional act. "I run straight to the goal with purpose in every step" (1 Cor. 9:26 LB). Paul had his destination in mind; he did not waste time, or energy, or effort. He observed the principle of intention.

I learned this lesson my first week on the tennis team in college. Some of us had developed bad habits while in high school. Some would throw their rackets if they were frustrated, slam balls into the fence if they missed a shot, or try trick shots just for the fun of it. After a week of these outbursts, our coach called a team meeting. "Let's get one thing straight. From this moment on, tennis is not a game; it is work. The objective is not to have fun and pass the time, but to win. In order to win, everything we do will have a purpose. When we run sprints it is to develop your speed, when we do drills it is to develop your agility, when we run distance it is to enhance your endurance. When you step out on the court, every ball you hit is to prepare you to perform at your maximum potential. If your actions do not promote your chances to win, don't do it. When you throw rackets and slam balls into the fence because you are upset and angry, it only wastes energy. Don't do anything that wastes your energy. You will need to conserve it for winning. We will win every match that goes into three sets simply because we are in better condition and have trained ourselves for that purpose."

My tennis coach must have been reading Paul's letter to the Corinthians. "I am like a boxer, who does not waste his punches" (1 Cor. 9:26 GNB).

To be intentional, we must ask a couple of questions. Will this activity help me reach my final destination? Does it enhance the priorities God has already established as my life's purpose?

## *Delay Gratification*

Paul wrote, "Every athlete goes into strict training . . . to win a fading wreath" (1 Cor. 9:25 NEB). Today, as in ancient times, Olympic athletes train for years in order to have the chance for a brief moment of glory. But the race we are running is far more important than any earthly athletic event.

The principle of delayed gratification is often expressed as "Save the best for last," "Do your homework first," "Pain now, pleasure later." M. Scott Peck described this tool of self-control as "a process of scheduling the pain and pleasure of life in such a way as to enhance the pleasure by meeting and experiencing the pain first and getting it over with." He adds, "It is the only decent way to live."[10]

As a college athlete I experienced the pain of wind sprints, the sheer agony of repetitive drills, and the utter drudgery of long distance running. Practice was like boot camp. Was it fun? No way! Was it worth it? You bet! All the sweat, pain, and aching muscles were minor compared to the benefit of personal triumph and of running for winning teams.

We can visualize delayed gratification in the athletic realm, but how does it function in the spiritual world, especially in the building of self-control? Often, delayed gratification involves routine daily choices. Skipping a late-night television program to go to bed early assures that one will be fresh in the morning for time with God. Determining to stand for your convictions protects you from falling into the pit of conformity. Pushing back from the table after a single helping of food enables a person to fit into clothes a size smaller. Attacking home chores and responsibilities soon after school or work leaves the rest of the evening to foster a relationship with your family.

At other times delayed gratification involves long-term resolutions. Abstaining from premarital sex will only make sex in marriage more beautiful. Spending twenty minutes a day with God will lead to a closer and more endearing relationship throughout life. Working very hard at your marriage at first— facing all conflicts and working through problem areas rather than letting them slide—will pay enormous dividends later.

The secret of such commitment involves enduring the suffering and anguish to enjoy the results. Football coaches have a favorite saying: "No pain, no gain." That is true in life. Many worthwhile endeavors in life are not fun. But when we get past the arduous drudgery, the reward is satisfaction.

While the rewards of self-control are great, they are seldom immediate. The writer of Hebrews told of individuals who patiently delayed gratification. The exciting chapter of faith, Hebrews 11, lists men and women who endured and suffered and agonized because they knew something better waited for them.

The author of the book closed chapter 11 by summarizing the lives of unsung heroes of faith.

> Some were laughed at and their backs cut open with whips, and others were chained in dungeons. Some died by stoning and some by being sawed in two; others were promised freedom if they would renounce their faith, then were killed with the sword. Some went about in skins of sheep and goats, wandering over deserts and mountains, hiding in dens and caves. They were hungry and sick and illtreated—too good for this world. (vv. 36–38 LB)

Why would people endure such hardship and distress? Why would they go on believing and preaching, knowing their lives were in danger? Why would they continue seeking to live a life pleasing to God when it incurred physical suffering? Why not give up, quit, call it off? The answer? "And these men of faith, though they trusted God and won his approval, none of them received all that God had promised them; for God wanted them to wait and share the even better rewards that were prepared for us" (vv. 39–40 LB).

Delayed gratification involves faith, and these saints knew it. Faith "is the certainty that what we hope for is waiting for us, even though we cannot see it up ahead" (v. 1 LB). We cannot see victory, but if we live believing in and practicing self-control, it will come. At present, all we may see are unwanted pounds, flabby muscles, an inconsistent walk with God, or defeating habits. But if we delay gratification, the desired result will eventually be reality. The payoff is worth the wait.

## Depend on Christ

If you want to develop self-control, learn to depend on Christ's power to help you. The most accurate and descriptive term for self-control is *Christ-control*. Self-control is not merely a self-produced behavior. "For God did not give us a spirit of timidity, but a spirit of power, of love and of self-discipline" (2 Tim. 1:7). God becomes the soul-stirring dynamic that enables us to gain that needed grip on our lives.

Christ-control, then, is the principle of submission. When we yield our inappropriate desires and passions to the Master, he provides the inner dynamic to help us defeat them. "Let the Spirit direct your lives, and you will not satisfy the desires of the human nature" (Gal. 5:16 GNB). God's unlimited power provides the needed strength to gain self-control. We can try all we want, but we have not utilized all the strength that is available to believers until we draw upon the Lord—the source of all strength.

A young boy was helping his father bring in some wood for the fire, and he was struggling under the weight of a heavy load. "Why don't you use all your strength?" the father asked. "I am," the little lad responded, feeling dejected. "No you're not," declared the father, "you have not asked me to help you." The father reached down and lifted up both the boy and the log in his arms. When we cast our burdens on the Lord, he will lift us up and sustain us.

Self-control has your best interests at heart. People exercising self-control are happier and healthier because they are fulfilling their inner potential. Many people never learn the joy of self-control, and consequently, they never reach their potential in any area of their lives.

The secret of self-control is Christ-control. If you still haven't done so, ask him to take control of your life right now. What a difference it will make in your life and for your character.

By the way, while writing this chapter, I completed refinishing that antique oak dresser. It's beautiful! Getting started again is the hardest part of completing any job. I discovered anew that once I begin working I really enjoy the project and am motivated to finish it.

# Chapter 6

# DEVELOPING THE ART
# OF PERSEVERANCE

. . . and to self-control, perseverance . . .
—2 Peter 1:6

We shall go on to the end, we shall fight in France,
    we shall fight on the seas and oceans,
We shall fight with growing confidence and
    growing strength in the air,
We shall defend our island, whatever the cost
    may be,
We shall fight on the beaches, we shall fight on the
    landing grounds,
We shall fight in the fields and in the streets, we
    shall fight in the hills;
We shall never surrender.[1]
    —Winston Churchill (4 June 1940)

On a commuter flight from Portland, Maine, to Boston in the summer of 1987, the pilot heard an unusual noise in the rear of the aircraft. Henry Dempsey turned the controls over to his copilot and went back to check it out. As he reached the tail section, the plane hit an air pocket, and Dempsey was tossed against the rear door. He quickly discovered the source of the mysterious noise.

The rear door had not been properly latched prior to takeoff and it fell open. Dempsey was instantly sucked out of the jet.

The copilot saw the red light on the control panel that indicated an open door, and he radioed the nearest airport, requesting permission to make an emergency landing. He reported that Dempsey had fallen out of the plane and requested that a helicopter be dispatched to search that area of the ocean.

After the plane landed, the ground crew found Henry Dempsey holding on to the outdoor ladder of the aircraft. Somehow, he had caught the ladder and managed to hold on for ten minutes as the plane flew two hundred miles per hour at an altitude of four thousand feet. What is more amazing, as the plane made its approach and landed, Dempsey had kept his head from hitting the runway, a mere twelve inches away. According to news reports, it took several airport personnel more than a few minutes to pry the pilot's fingers from the ladder.

That is a picture of perseverance—the ability to hang on when it would have been easier to let go. Many people are blessed with certain attributes, but persistence is foremost for success in any endeavor. Persistence is the key that keeps us from giving up and letting go.

*Webster's New Ideal Dictionary* defines *persevere* as "to keep at something in spite of difficulties, opposition, or discouragement."[2] Popular colloquial phrases for perseverance include "Keep on keeping on," "Hang in there," "Put up with it," "Stick-to-itiveness." Its synonyms are determination, endurance, tenacity, stamina, and backbone. When *perseverance* is used in the Bible it means to abide under, to bear up courageously, and to tarry or wait.

Henry Dempsey would just say perseverance is holding on for dear life.

Perseverance, too, is an attitude that challenges us to plod ahead in spite of adversity. It causes us to remain faithful under trials and tests in a way that honors God. It produces an inner dynamic that enables us not to be resigned to difficulties. It is a quiet confidence in God, knowing that he is in control. It says, "I can hold on a little longer because I know that God is going to work all things for his good." It is having the patience to let God do his work in his time. All God asks is that we hold on a little longer.

Perseverance is our responsibility—not God's. Productivity is God's responsibility—not ours. Perseverance holds on to the hope and the promise that God is working in and through us to fashion a distinguished life. It sustains moral excellence. It turns our knowledge of God into a life that reflects his character. It gives stamina to self-control so we will perform the needed disciplines to live distinctively.

## The Power of Perseverance

The race is not always won by the fastest. The game is not always won by the strongest. Rather, it is won by the person who keeps hanging on and refuses to let go. Consider the postage stamp. Its usefulness consists in its ability to stick to one thing until it gets there. Consider the words of race car driver Rick Mears: "To finish first you must first finish."[3] The late Ray Kroc, founder of the world-famous McDonald's hamburger chain, lived the same statement that football coach Vince Lombardi often quoted: "Press on: nothing in the world can take the place of persistence. Talent will not; nothing is more common than unsuccessful individuals with talent. Genius will not; unrewarded genius is almost a proverb. Education will not; the world is full of educated derelicts. Persistence and determination alone are omnipotent."[4]

Never underestimate the incredible power of persistence. It was the power that enabled Henry Dempsey to cling to an airplane ladder for ten minutes while traveling two hundred miles per hour at four thousand feet. It makes things possible. T. F. Buxton said, "I hold a doctrine to which I owe much, indeed, but all the little I ever had, namely, that with ordinary talent and extraordinary perseverance, all things are attainable."[5]

## The Priority of Perseverance

The Bible considers perseverance a priority. Paul expressed its importance in character development: "Not only so, but we also rejoice in our sufferings, because we know that suffering produces perseverance; perseverance, character; and character, hope. And hope does not disappoint us, because God has poured out his love into our hearts by the Holy Spirit, whom he has given us" (Rom. 5:3–5). The writer of Hebrews also knew that perseverance was mandatory in the pursuit of character: "You need to persevere so that when you have done the will of God, you will receive what he has promised" (Heb. 10:36). God demonstrates great patience and persistence toward the world in general and toward disobedient disciples in particular. "The Lord is not slow in keeping his promise, as some understand slowness. He is patient with you, not wanting anyone to perish, but everyone to come to repentance" (2 Peter 3:9). Since persistence is a key characteristic of God, we must grow in our ability to hold on in order to reflect his image.

The following principles will enable you to develop perseverance. All are rooted in our relationship with and our understanding of God.

## Accept the Unchangeable

William Barclay described perseverance as "the courageous acceptance of everything life can do to us and the transmitting of even the worst event into another step on the upward way." Some events and circumstances are, of course, inevitable. Sometimes life isn't fair; sometimes we're faced with injustices. Sometimes we fall, metaphorically, out of unlocked airplane doors. Accept those things that cannot be changed.

It helps to remember that God is in charge of our lives. He desires that we grow in the likeness of his Son. So whatever enters our lives—unfavorable circumstances, tragic events, or irritating people—is for the development of character. Be it good, bad, or indifferent, our response to life's irritants forms our character.

The oyster illustrates a positive response to life's irritants. When an alien substance—a grain of sand—slips inside the oyster's shell, all of the oyster's resources are concentrated on releasing healing fluids, which otherwise would have remained dormant. Eventually the irritant is covered and the wound healed, forming a pearl. The pearl, therefore, is a product of stress. The precious jewel is conceived through irritation, born of adversity. Had there been no wounding, no irritating intrusion, there would have been no pearl.

J. B. Phillips understood the value derived from overcoming life's irritants, and that understanding is evident in his paraphrase of James 1:2–4: "When all kinds of trials and temptations crowd into your lives, my brothers, don't resent them as intruders, but welcome them as friends! Realize that they come to test your faith and to produce in you the quality of endurance. But let the process go on until that endurance is fully developed, and you will find you have become men [and women] of mature character."

Talking about accepting adversity, though, is often easier than living through it. After having been out of college for several years, I decided to return to graduate school to work on a Ph.D. The school asked me to complete a master's degree before I entered the doctoral program. For one academic year I sweated and slaved, researching, writing, and studying to complete the master's degree. I knew that if I passed the course I would gain entrance into the Ph.D. program, my ultimate objective. On the day I defended (and passed) my master's thesis, I was informed that my application to the doctoral program had been rejected.

For several years my wife and I had planned, saved, and given up so much to fulfill this lifelong dream. Now the dream was shattered. Many times I had counseled people with the words,

"Life isn't fair." When I swallowed them, they went down hard, and very bitter.

At times life hands us a raw deal. We are promised the sweet, but must swallow the bitter. We hope for happiness, but receive suffering. We long for comfort, but face adversity.

My disappointment, though deeply felt, doesn't compare to the tragedies experienced by many other people. It was, nonetheless, painful. What, though, could I learn from the pain? Aldous Huxley said, "Experience is not what happens to a man; it's what a man does with what happens to him."[6] I could hang on to my bitterness or I could squeeze knowledge and wisdom from the experience.

I was, in the end, able to say, "I turn this over to you, Lord. Life may not be fair, but I know you are. I accept your wisdom in allowing this to happen. I claim your sovereignty in my life. I accept your perfect timing in allowing what happened. I may not understand it all but I accept your plan. I accept that the best you can give me is not changed circumstances but a relationship with you through your Son. I accept the fact that you are working through and in my life."

## Adjust to the Obstacles

Solomon wrote, "A prudent man foresees the difficulties ahead and prepares for them; the simpleton goes blindly on and suffers the consequences" (Prov. 22:3 LB). Some circumstances are unavoidable; disappointments and obstacles are a certainty; we will likely face losses. The person with perseverance acknowledges the road blocks and makes adjustments. Thomas Carlyle noted, "The block of granite that was an obstacle in the pathway of the weak becomes a stepping stone in the pathway of the strong."[7]

When the obstacles of life are stacked before us we can adjust by going around, climbing over, or tunneling under. People who don't adjust wind up bitter and disillusioned, never fulfilled as persons. They just keep chipping away at the granite wall.

Not far from my childhood home in Alabama is a row of maple trees. Some fifty years ago, a farmer planted the maples around the perimeter of a three-acre pasture. Then some time later, when the maples were large enough, the farmer used them as fence posts. Old barbed wire is still strung between each mature tree. I'm sure it was a trauma for the young trees to have barbed wire hammered into their tender bark. I noticed that the barbed wire had been accepted and incorporated by some of the trees but not by others. Some fought it. Others adjusted.

The trees that did not adjust were severely disfigured by the wire. They became its victims. But others showed no marks at all. The wire simply entered one side and emerged on the other—almost as if it had been inserted by a drill bit. Those trees mastered the wire.

Are you allowing intrusions to distort and disfigure your life? Are you trying to change circumstances or people in your life? Why not transform these obstacles into building blocks by learning to adjust?

What if Joseph had not been enslaved in Egypt? His family would have starved many years later. If John Bunyan had not been imprisoned we probably would not have his classic *Pilgrim's Progress*. If Phillips Brooks had not failed as a schoolteacher he would not have produced his beautiful sermons or written inspiring hymns like "O Little Town of Bethlehem." At age forty-six, German composer Ludwig van Beethoven became completely deaf. Nevertheless, he wrote his greatest music, including five symphonies, during his later years. Louis L'Amour wrote over one hundred western novels, selling over two hundred million copies. But he received three hundred fifty rejections before he made his first sale. When we adjust to the detours of life, God reveals some of his marvelous handiwork off the beaten trail. Don't think of adjustment as failure, think of it as education.

Hang on; see what God has in store for you around the next bend.

## Abide with Patience

Someone once said, "You can do anything if you have patience. You can carry water in a sieve—if you wait until it freezes." Unfortunately, most of us aren't that patient. When we need it, we usually pray, "Lord, give me patience . . . and I want it now." Or as former British Prime Minister Margaret Thatcher said more eloquently, "I am extraordinarily patient provided I get my own way in the end."[8]

But one can't learn patience by listening to a sermon (unless, of course, the sermon is so long one must practice patience in order to stay until the end). Nor can one learn patience by reading a book (unless the book is so boring it requires patience just to finish it). The only way to learn patience is by taking life as it comes—holding on, gritting your teeth, and riding out the storm. And that's not easy. Sitting in God's waiting room is perhaps the most difficult aspect of the Christian experience.

In the Greek language, the term for patience is often translated "long-suffering." In Greek, it's a compound word. The first part means "long or far"; the second part means "hot, anger, or wrath." With the parts together, the word literally means "long-anger." In English we have an expression, *short-tempered*. We would not miss the Greek meaning very far if we called patience *long-tempered*. Patience prevents us from blowing up when events don't go our way or losing our cool when others upset us.

Believers are exhorted to display patience. James wrote, "Be patient, then, brothers, until the Lord's coming. See how the farmer waits for the land to yield its valuable crop and how patient he is for the autumn and spring rains. You too, be patient and stand firm, because the Lord's coming is near" (James 5:7–8). A farmer, indeed, demonstrates patience. A farmer cannot make it rain or produce growth, but must rely on God to act in the most wise and merciful way.

Patiently enduring the adversity and struggles of life is not fun. It doesn't seem to be rewarding at the time. But in the end it does develop character. As a child I was told, "Just be patient." The same thing holds true for adults. When we wait on God's timing we become stronger.

A man once found a cocoon on a tree in his yard. He was intrigued by it and decided to watch it change. One day, he saw a tiny butterfly inside the delicate covering. It struggled, trying its best to break out of the cocoon. Finally, the man became so frustrated that he used a razor blade to make a tiny slit in the side of the cocoon in order to free the struggling butterfly. Soon afterward, the butterfly was free, but it hadn't developed the strength to fly. It died prematurely. As we wait patiently through the struggles of life we obtain strength.

The secret of patience is abiding. The term rendered *perseverance* in James 5:11 literally means "to abide under." We must learn to rest and endure under the load of pain and suffering by abiding with God, who is faithful. We not only abide *in* Christ but also abide *with* Christ under the struggles and the pressures of life.

## Affix Your Eyes on the Prize

The problem with experiencing frustrations and delays is that we lose sight of the final goal. But when we attach ourselves to our reason for living—a life resembling that of Christ's—we are able to persevere.

Paul stated to the Corinthians, "For our light and momentary troubles are achieving for us an eternal glory that far outweighs them all. So we fix our eyes not on what is seen, but on what is unseen. For what is seen is temporary, but what is unseen is eternal" (2 Cor. 4:17–18). To keep our eyes fixed on the unseen, we need Christ's perspective. The writer of Hebrews used Jesus as our example: "Let us run with perseverance the race marked out for us. Let us fix our eyes on Jesus, the author and perfecter of our faith, who for the joy set before him endured the cross, scorning its shame, and sat down at the right hand of the throne of God. Consider him who endured such opposition from sinful men, so that you will not grow weary and lose heart" (Heb. 12:1–3).

Our troubles are minimal; our hurts fade in comparison to the final prize. Our gaze must constantly be focused on Christ. And when we keep our eyes on the goal we will be motivated to continue on.

Psychologists refer to two kinds of personal motivation—external and internal. External motivation reveals itself in punishment, pain, or reward. It works only as long as the external stimulus is present. Take away the stimulus and the motivation is diminished. Internal motivation comes from self-esteem, self-actualization, or pride. Whereas external motivation is superficial, internal motivation is more powerful and produces longer lasting results. Of the two, external or internal, psychologists insist that internal is the best and most effective.

The apostle Paul, however, reveals a third kind of motivation, one that is even more powerful and enduring than the previous two. Paul speaks of fixing our eyes on "eternal" motivation. In the end, that which is internal and external will disappear; only that which is eternal will last. The motivation that lasts a lifetime and beyond is inspired by Christ.

The hymn, "When We All Get to Heaven," describes eternal motivation:

> While we walk the pilgrim pathway
> Clouds will overspread the sky;
> But when traveling days are over
> Not a shadow, not a sigh.

Let us then be true and faithful,
Trusting, serving every day;
Just one glimpse of Him in glory
Will the toils of life repay.

Why do you do what you do? The *why's* of life often determine the *how long's* of life. Are your pursuits for the temporal or the eternal? Are your struggles for the here-and-now or for the life above? If you want to develop staying power, live for eternal priorities. When everything we do is done for Jesus' sake and for heaven's reward, we will never lack staying power.

## Affirm the Presence

As we work to build a distinctive life we must always remember that God is with us. Sometimes God is like a teacher, instructing us in the task at hand. Sometimes God is a fellow worker, challenging us to excellence. Sometimes God is a spectator, encouraging us to keep on keeping on. In whatever situation we find ourselves, God is always with us.

I recall long and grueling basketball practices in high school. The gym was not air-conditioned. We would run, it seemed, forever. My legs throbbed, my heart pounded, and my side felt like it would split. I wanted to quit. But then something wonderful would happen. My body would provide a miraculous, gracious replenishing of energy known as a second wind.

As we run toward a life of distinctive character we will experience something similar. Getting started poses no problem, but we get bogged down as the race continues. A time comes when our personal resources are exhausted. Yet as we persevere, God seems to give us a spiritual second wind.

Isaiah described this miracle: "Do you not know? Have you not heard? The LORD is the everlasting God, the Creator of the ends of the earth. He will not grow tired or weary, and his understanding no one can fathom. He gives strength to the weary and increases the power of the weak. Even youths grow tired and weary, and young men stumble and fall; but those who hope in the LORD will renew their strength. They will soar on wings like eagles; they will run and not grow weary, they will walk and not be faint" (Isa. 40:28–31).

The secret to spiritual replenishment is found in affirming God's presence. The world says give up, drop out, run away. God says, "Trust me, lean on me, and fall into my arms." God is with you to support and sustain you. To give you hope, courage, and strength to continue. He has promised, "My Presence will go with you, and I will give you rest" (Exod. 33:14).

Ignance Paderewski, Poland's famous concert pianist and prime minister, was giving a series of concerts, according to a popular story. A mother, wishing to encourage her young son's progress at the piano, bought tickets for a performance. When the night arrived, mother and son found their seats near the front of the concert hall and eyed the majestic Steinway waiting on stage. The mother spotted a friend in the audience and walked down the aisle to greet her. Seizing the opportunity to explore the wonders of the concert hall, the little boy eventually made his way through a door marked, "No Admittance." When the house lights dimmed and the concert was about to begin, the mother returned to her seat and discovered that the child was missing.

Suddenly, the curtains parted and spotlights focused on the impressive Steinway on stage. In horror, the mother saw her little boy sitting at the keyboard, innocently picking out, "Twinkle, Twinkle, Little Star." His mother gasped, but before she could retrieve her son, the great piano master appeared on the stage and quickly moved to the keyboard. He whispered to the boy, "Don't quit—keep playing." Leaning over, Paderewski reached down with his left hand and began filling in a bass part. Soon, his right arm reached around the other side, encircling the child, to add a running obbligato. Together, the old master and young novice held the crowd mesmerized.

In our quest for a distinctive character, unpolished and incomplete though we may be, it is the Master who surrounds us and whispers in our ears, time and again, "Don't quit—keep playing." And as we do, he augments and supplements until a work of amazing beauty is created. What we can accomplish on our own is hardly noteworthy. We try our best but the results are less than memorable. But with the hand of the Master, our characters can be resplendent. Our responsibility is to not quit, to keep playing; his part is to fashion a masterpiece.

Remember, God doesn't call the equipped; he equips the called. And he'll always be there to love and to guide you to great things.

Are you close to quitting? Please don't do it. Are you tired of trying to live for Christ? Hold on. Do you feel like giving up on this pursuit toward a distinctive character? Roll up your sleeves and get back in there. Can't resist temptation? Accept God's forgiveness and keep on living rightly. Do you feel that sorrow and disappointment greet you every morning? Hang in there. God is there with you.

## Those Who Persist Prevail

Perseverance prevails. "Blessed is the man who perseveres under trial, because when he has stood the test, he will receive the crown of life that God has promised to those who love him" (James 1:12). Remember, you are not a failure until you give up. You won't fall until you let go.

In the quest for distinctive character, it does not matter where you start but that you finish. In a ball game the most meaningless statistic is the half time score. Those who persist prevail. Consider the oak tree—a little nut that refused to give up its ground, or the snail who made it to Noah's ark—he just kept going and going and going.

During the 1890s Gentleman "Jim" (James John) Corbett held the heavyweight boxing title of the world for five years. Corbett once said to would-be champion boxers:

Fight one more round. When your feet are so tired that you have to shuffle back to the center of the ring, fight one more round. When your arms are so tired that you can hardly lift your hands to come on guard, fight one more round. When your nose is bleeding and your eyes are black and you are so tired that you wish your opponent would crack you on the jaw and put you to sleep, fight one more round—remembering that the man who fights one more round is never whipped.[9]

The fact remains that we will be buffeted and plummeted, attacked and assaulted. We will stagger and fall. But we must fight one more round. We must rise each time we fall.

The poem "The Race" describes a young boy who ran a race, falling many times, yet finishing. One stanza reads:

> And to his dad he sadly said,
> "I didn't do too well."
> "To me, you won," his father said.
> "You rose each time you fell."[10]

So don't quit. Never give up. Keep going. Hold on. God's rewards await us in the future; we don't know how many steps it will take to reach the prize. No breaks or time-outs exist; we must work every day of our lives. It has been said, "Life is like reading a book. It begins to make sense when we near the end." Perseverance provides the stamina needed to see the end and embrace the prize. So fight another round, rise another time and, above all, like Henry Dempsey, don't let go.

*Chapter 7*

# RADIATING THE AURA
# OF GODLINESS

. . . and to perseverance, godliness . . .

—2 Peter 1:6

Godliness is this: the quality of life, that when people
are around you, they think of God.[1]

—Vernon Grounds

When my daughter, Bailey, was in the fourth grade her class
learned to spell new words each week. As a part of that learning
exercise her teacher had the students write sentences using each
word. One week one of the words was *heritage*. The night before
Bailey handed in her sentences I was proofreading her assign-
ment. For *heritage*, she wrote, "My mom and dad are Christians
so I am a part of a godly heritage." My eyes moistened as I read
that sentence. Somewhere along the way she had come to understand that godliness was a pursuit of her parents. (And I hope it
will be her pursuit, too.)

A Christian can receive no greater compliment than to be referred to as a godly person. A person may be zealous, talented, a
leader; but none of these matter if he or she is not growing in
godliness.

The words *godly* and *godliness* appear only a few times in the

New Testament, yet the entire Bible is a book on godliness. When
these words do appear they are saturated with meaning.

Godliness is not an option in the development of a distinctive
character. The apostle Peter instructs us, add to "perseverance,
godliness" (2 Peter 1:6). Godliness is not reserved for a few quaint
Christians of a bygone era or for some group of super saints of
today. The privilege and duty of every Christian is to pursue godliness, to study and practice godliness. And to attain this goal we
don't need any special talent or equipment. God "has given us
everything we need for life and godliness" (2 Peter 1:3). He has
planted the seed of godliness; we are to see that it germinates,
grows, and blossoms.

But what is godliness? What does it mean to be godly? Do we
have to live in a monastery to be godly? Does it mean we can't
watch television? Can a person be godly and yet competitive and
lucrative in business? Godliness is not what a person does or
how a person looks or what a person owns. Many of us make
judgments on the basis of exterior appearances, but godliness
goes beyond the facade. Godliness is more than skin deep—it is
the religion of the heart. Godliness resides deep in a believer's
life, affecting everything he or she does and is—his or her behavior and character. Godly character moves beyond morality, be-
nevolence, and zeal. A person may be talented, involved in God's
work, and even successful in some aspect of Christian service
and still not be godly. A godly life possesses a new dimension
that reflects the qualities of God. Following are the distinctive
marks of a godly man or woman. I hope it was these characteristics that my daughter saw in my life.

## Taking God Seriously

The godly person is sensitive, respectful, and reverent toward
God and the things of God. All things are seen in relationship to
God. Not that godly people are serious-minded at all times. They

enjoy life because they enjoy the creator of life. They know him. They listen to him. They are devoted to him. They have a relationship with him, and they walk humbly with him. They reverence him and hold him in awe. They understand and fear his majesty and power. And anything—anything—that has God's name in front of it—God's Word, God's house, God's day, God's will—is held in reverence.

The Old Testament tells of a people who failed to take God seriously. God rescued the ancient Hebrews from slavery and oppression in Egypt. On their journey home to Israel they witnessed the miracles of God: He delivered them through the Red Sea and from their Egyptian pursuers; he guided them with a cloud by day and a pillar of fire by night; he provided nourishment with manna from heaven and water from rocks. God's workings were thus constantly evident. These people, surrounded by unparalleled privileges, had everything. God's leader, Moses, was out in front of them, and God's own presence was constant. The Hebrew nation had been given a heritage of godliness. In fact, one would think that these people would be the epitome of godliness. But they were not. The apostle Paul wrote of them, "Nevertheless, God was not pleased with most of them; their bodies were scattered over the desert" (1 Cor. 10:5).

Why was God not pleased? What happened to these potential saints? What caused their downfall? As they journeyed from Egypt they played games with their lives and with God.

And that is dangerous business.

Paul, again, summarizes their tragedy: "The people sat down to eat and drink, and stood up to play" (1 Cor. 10:7 NASB), or "indulge in pagan revelry" (v. 7 NIV). It sounded like a fraternity party. The supernatural became commonplace. God-talk abounded, but the people lacked reverence and awe for God. They became callous to the divine, nonchalant in their values. Because they forgot their heritage they grew apathetic in regard to their privileged position as God's chosen people. They did not mean business with God, and their relationship with him became a farce.

Sound familiar? Think about what is happening today in the United States. Never in the history of the world has one country been so blessed. We are inundated with churches, Christian radio and television, Christian magazines and books, Christian schools, Christian conferences and seminars. Never has there been such potential for religious instruction. Our churches should be overflowing with godly men and women. But all too often we walk down the same paths of carnality as the ancient Hebrews. We make light of what we should honor. We wink at what we should weep about. We play at what we should take seriously.

Do you take God seriously? If you do, you are well on your way to godliness.

Jack returned to his hometown after being away for many years. As he looked around at familiar faces and places, he noticed that the old church where he had once worshiped no longer existed. He asked the man who had operated the service station since Jack was a child, "What ever happened to that old church and the glory it once had?"

The attendant asked him, "Are you going to be driving around town some more today?"

Jack replied, "Yes."

The attendant said, "If you drive up the hill where the church used to stand, you'll see a sign. Read it carefully. It'll tell you what happened to that old church and its glory."

Later in the evening Jack started up the hill. It was getting dark, so he slowed down to catch the message written on the sign. As his headlights glared on it, Jack read these words: "Drive Carefully: Children at Play."[2]

Do you take God seriously or do you merely play at the things of God? Is your religion of the heart or is it superficial, skin-deep? Do you speak the Christian lingo, but fail to live the life of godliness?

Be careful, that is dangerous business.

What happens when people play with God? What happens when people fail to take God seriously?

Achan's story is in Joshua 7. He's the Israelite who, in direct opposition to the decree of God, took spoils for himself from the conquest of Canaan. Because of Achan's sin, the army of Israel lost the next battle at Ai. Joshua confronted Achan. Even though he confessed his sin, punishment for Achan and his family was stoning.

The people of Sodom and Gomorrah suffered a similar consequence. Their story is told in Genesis 18–19. God informed Abraham that if ten righteous people could be found there, the cities would be spared destruction. Because even a mere ten people who took God seriously could not be found, the cities were destroyed.

Acts 5 tells of two members during the infancy of the church. Ananias and Sapphira schemed to withhold money promised to the church in Jerusalem. They lied to Peter and the Holy Spirit, saying that the money they were giving was the total amount they had received from the sale of their land. In fact it was not, and they were struck dead.

Not taking God seriously is dangerous business.

## Imitating God

To describe godliness merely as an attitude is insufficient. The description must go a step further. The original meaning of the New Testament word for *godliness* conveys the idea of a personal attitude toward God that results in actions that are pleasing to him. In fact, the simplest definition of godliness is God-likeness.

When I think of God I think of his love, his forgiveness, his mercy, his salvation, and his offer of redemption. The word *godly* is an adjective, and thus describes how our actions should resemble God's actions. A life of godliness, therefore, takes on a dimension that reflects the very stamp of God.

The apostle Paul's letter to the church at Ephesus says, "Be imitators of God, therefore, as dearly loved children and live a life of love, just as Christ loved us and gave himself up for us as a fragrant offering and sacrifice to God" (Eph. 5:1–2). In other words, we are to act like God. We are to copy his character, emulate his movements, and replicate his personality.

A believer can fill his or her schedule with activities of a religious nature, but his or her heart may be far from God. The instructions for achieving godliness do not mandate a quota of religious activities. Instead, we are instructed to display behaviors that are most like God: love, giving, and sacrifice. Isn't this the same conduct demonstrated by God when he sent Jesus to this world? "For God so loved the world that he gave his one and only Son" (John 3:16). God *loved* us so much that he *gave* his only Son, who *sacrificed* himself on a cruel Roman cross for our sin.

Do your love, your giving, and your sacrifice remind people of God?

Inside of most Christians is a deep-seated desire to love rather than to hate, to release rather than to grasp, to give of themselves rather than to keep for themselves. This is the essence of Christianity, and most importantly, the summation of godly action.

Shortly after the conclusion of World War II, Europe began picking up the pieces. Much of the Old Country had been ravaged by war and lay in ruins. Perhaps the saddest sight of all was that of little orphaned children starving in the streets of those war-torn cities.

Early one chilly morning an American soldier was making his way back to the barracks in London. As he turned the corner in his jeep, he spotted a little lad with his nose pressed to the window of a pastry shop. Inside, the cook was kneading dough for a fresh batch of doughnuts. The hungry boy stared in silence, watching every move. The soldier pulled his jeep to the curb, stopped, got out, and walked quietly over to where the little fellow was standing. Through the steamed-up window he could see the mouth-watering morsels as they were being pulled from the oven, piping hot. The boy salivated and released a slight groan as he watched the cook place them ever so carefully onto the glass-enclosed counter.

The soldier's heart went out to the nameless orphan beside him.

"Son, would you like some of those?"

The boy was startled. "Oh, yeah. I would!"

The American stepped inside and bought a dozen, put them in a bag, and walked back to where the lad waited in the fog and the cold. He smiled, held out the bag, and said simply, "Here you are."

As he turned to walk away, he felt a tug on his coat. He looked back and the child ask quietly, "Mister, are you God?"[3]

We are never more like God than when we love, and when we give, and when we sacrifice for others.

Godliness is a life of obedience. God commands us to love, therefore, we love. God commands us to give, therefore, we give. God commands us to sacrifice, therefore, we sacrifice. Paying lip service to God is not acceptable; talk is cheap. Heart-felt actions devoted to God are essential.

## Attractiveness That Looks Like God

A friend came running up to me after church one Sunday. Excitedly, she told me her story.

Her boss at work stopped her at the copier that week and said, "I want what you got."

"What do you mean?" she asked.

He went on, "I admire your joy, your graciousness, your outlook on life, your attitude toward difficulties, and your love and forgiveness of others. Where does it come from?"

"Wow," I said, "that's quite a compliment."

My friend went on to tell her boss that she hadn't always been that way. Two years before, she had become a Christian, and she had been studying and learning and growing in relationship with

God ever since. It was God's life and nature and character flooding out of her life that made the difference.

A sad fact of Christianity today is that our churches are full of professing Christians who claim to know God, but who are not attracting people to Christianity. We are sad and depressed, and our demeanor is ugly. We look like we have been weaned on dill pickles. Instead of being ambassadors in the world, we are an embarrassment to the church.

Has God failed? No. We haven't done the work to edify and beautify ourselves. Becoming godly is akin to a bride getting ready for her wedding day. The bride takes great measures, many months in advance, to project her most beautiful self on her wedding day. Similar steps need to be taken by Christians as we prepare for "The Day" when Jesus returns to take his bride, "The Church," home with him.

In the Old Testament, the nation of Israel was the Bride. In the New Testament, the church is the Bride. As members of God's family, we are to be growing in godliness so that we will become beautiful people. I'm not talking about external beauty, even though the edification process will affect our countenances and our outlooks. I'm referring to an inward attractiveness that radiates the presence of Christ in our lives. Beautiful people radiate. The more time we spend in the presence of God the more we radiate the likeness of God. Consider Moses when he descended from Mount Sinai after spending forty days with God. Or Jesus after being transfigured on the mountainside in the presence of God. Godly people radiate the character of Christ. Godly habits take root and the believer increases in his or her likeness to the Master. An aura of inviting warmth radiates from the person committed to godliness.

## Reminds People of God

The sense of smell can be a powerful memory prod. A mere sniff of a certain odor can transport you back to another time and place, reminding you of some event or person long since forgotten. Diesel fumes remind me of chartering busloads of youth to the ski slopes of Colorado. One whiff of those fumes and I am immediately transported back to the powder trails of a majestic mountain.

The apostle Paul wrote to the Corinthians, "But thanks be to God, who always leads us in triumphal procession in Christ and through us spreads everywhere the fragrance of the knowledge of him. For we are to God the aroma of Christ among those who are being saved and those who are perishing. To the one we are the smell of death; to the other, the fragrance of life" (2 Cor. 2:14–16).

In Paul's day the "Roman Triumph" was like a present-day American "ticker-tape" parade for a hero or champion. This spectacle was the special tribute that Rome gave to its conquering generals. The procession would include the commander in chief in a golden chariot, surrounded by his officers. The parade would display the spoils of battle, as well as the captive enemy soldiers. The Roman priests would also be in the parade, carrying burning incense to pay tribute to the victorious army.

The passage above from 2 Corinthians refers to a similar picture, but with Jesus—who has defeated the enemy, Satan—leading the procession and with us—his army—sharing in the victory. But believers are to do more than follow Jesus; we are to be God's fragrance to the world, a constant aroma, reminding the world of Jesus' victory and his wonder-working power. Godly people, then, are the incense of Christianity, and godliness makes us burn, releasing the fragrance of God and his work in our lives. This aroma distinguishes us as we let the fragrance of Jesus permeate our lives.

## The Means to Godliness

How do the attitudes, actions, attractiveness, and aroma of godliness permeate our lives? In other words, how do we radiate the aura of godliness?

## *Thirst*

First, godly people thirst for God. We are instructed "to say 'No' to ungodliness and worldly passions, and to live . . . godly lives in this present age" (Titus 2:12) until the return of Christ. If we want to be godly we must long for God.

David vividly expressed his longing: "As the deer pants for streams of water, so my soul pants for you, O God. My soul thirsts for God, for the living God. When can I go and meet with God?" (Ps. 42:1–2). What could be more intense than a hunted deer's thirst for water? The psalmist yearned to see the face of God, to enter into his fellowship and presence.

On another occasion David expressed this desire for God. "One thing I ask of the LORD, this is what I seek: that I may dwell in the house of the LORD all the days of my life, to gaze upon the beauty of the LORD and to seek him in his temple" (27:4). Then again David wrote, "O God, you are my God, earnestly I seek you; my soul thirsts for you, my body longs for you, in a dry and weary land where there is no water" (63:1). More than for anything else David thirsted for God. Is it any wonder that God said of him, "I have found David son of Jesse a man after my own heart; he will do everything I want him to do" (Acts 13:22)?

The relationship with God can be compared with dating and marriage. The lovers cherish the first weeks and months together. They can't wait to see each other, to be with each other, and to share each other's company. They long and thirst for one another, each earnestly desiring to know everything about the other. Then they get married. The excitement and longing soon wear off, and they begin to take one another for granted.

Is your present relationship with God similar? Have you lost the spark? Do you no longer hunger and thirst for God?

That yearning, the thirsting for God, comes through effort. Paul instructed Timothy to "pursue . . . godliness" (1 Tim. 6:11). The word rendered *pursue* embodies unrelenting or persevering effort. The need for perseverance has been discussed in chapter 6. It is now clear why perseverance is important. Without it we will never be godly. Intensity of longing for God is the heartbeat of a godly person.

Columnist Herb Caen wrote in the *San Francisco Chronicle,* "Every morning in Africa, a gazelle wakes up. It knows it must run faster than the fastest lion or it will be killed. Every morning a lion wakes up. It knows it must outrun the slowest gazelle or it will starve to death." Caen surmised, "It doesn't matter whether you are a lion or a gazelle; when the sun comes up, you'd better be running."[4] In other words, in the jungle passivity is not conducive to survival. Neither is passivity conducive to godliness.

Charles Spurgeon, famed British preacher of the late 1800s, wrote, "If you are not seeking the Lord, the Devil is seeking you. If you are not seeking the Lord, judgment is at your heels."[5]

In pursuit of godliness, then, it's not enough to simply wake up. We are called to run, to become like Christ, to press ahead to godliness. Godliness doesn't come by sitting passively, waiting for it to drop into our laps. It requires hard work, perseverance, and continual effort. In a manner of speaking, you have to run for it with everything you've got. The godly person is content in his or her relationship with God, but never satisfied with the present experience. The godly person always yearns for more.

How can we quench our thirst for God? Only one way exists. It is by spending time with God. I don't know of a single godly man or woman who doesn't spend time daily with God. It is impossible to develop godliness without taking the time to develop a deeper relationship with God. We cannot please God without walking with him and developing a relationship with him.

## Focus

Second, godly people focus on God. The pursuer of godliness focuses attention on God in all things. Modern culture tends to divert our focus away from God, making it quite possible to become an idolater. An idol is anything that draws our attention and adoration away from God. In the apostle's letter to Timothy, the subject of godliness is discussed in reference to two distractions from its pursuit. Both have a focus on self. The first was physical exercise: "Have nothing to do with godless myths and old wives' tales; rather, train yourself to be godly. For physical training is of some value, but godliness has value for all things, holding promise for both the present life and the life to come" (1 Tim. 4:7–8). The second was money: "But godliness with contentment is great gain. . . . For the love of money is a root of all kinds of evil. Some people, eager for money, have wandered from the faith and pierced themselves with many griefs. But you, man of God, flee from all this, and pursue righteousness, godliness . . ." (1 Tim. 6:6, 10–11).

It is ironic that Paul correctly addresses the problem of many twentieth-century Americans. The age of physical fitness and monetary gain are upon us, and idolatry often takes the form of pursuing affluence or a gym-buffed physique. There's nothing inherently sinful in these pursuits—until they come between God and us.

A man who had spent all of his time making and hoarding money found himself in a most disturbed and unhappy state. He went to a minister for counsel.

The minister, who knew the man rather well, picked up the Bible, pointed to the word "God," and asked, "Can you see that?"

"Certainly," replied the man with annoyance.

"All right," said the minister as he picked up a coin and placed it over the word *God*. "Can you see the word now?"

The man did not immediately reply, but eventually he said, "Yes, I understand now."

Jerry Bridges noted that "godliness is an exercise or discipline that focuses upon God."[6] What are you doing to focus on God? Have you allowed the cares and worries of the world to blur your vision of God? What activities are you performing to keep your-self spiritually fit?

## *Worship*

Third, godly people worship God. Note the progression in the previous points. Craving evil things leads to idolatry, which leads to immorality. On the other hand, thirsting for God leads to fo-cusing on God, which leads to worshiping God.

Focusing on self causes immorality; worshiping God is to prop-erly acknowledge him. We see him as he is—majestic and sover-eign—and we see ourselves as we are—finite and helpless. The godly person removes him- or herself from the center of his or her world and puts God in his proper place. In fact, the Greek word rendered *godliness* embodies the idea of worship rightly directed.

Reverence for God will cause our worship to be rightly directed. A church in my city advertises one of its worship services with the sign, "Casual Worship." They are, of course, communicating to motorists that their worship service is informal and welcomes casual dress. But the first time I saw their sign, I wanted to stop and say, "There is nothing casual about worship." Far too often, we take God lightly. We approach him in a trite and casual fash-ion. We think of God as our buddy or our pal. But he is the eternal God of the universe, who has a claim on our lives be-cause he has placed eternity within our hearts. We are to approach him with respect and reverence.

Reverence of God will also regulate our conduct. John Murray says, "What or whom we worship determines our behavior."[7] If a man worships basketball his conduct and behavior is consumed with the sport. If a woman worships money she is driven to ac-cumulate as much as possible. If a person worships God, he or she seeks to know him and live obediently to his principles.

## *Serve*

Fourth, godly people serve other people. Godly people don't whine and complain about what's happening to them. Instead, they find joy in service. The best way to de-emphasize personal misfortune is to get involved with those who are less fortunate. In doing so, you'll discover that you're better off than most.

The godly individual not only gives God his due, but also serves others and gives them their due. Someone said, "Some people are so heavenly minded they are no earthly good." On the contrary, it is only when people *are* heavenly minded that they can be of any earthly good. As we invest time with God he will guide us to serve others. Godly people know that service is an outgrowth of worship.

The best evidence of godliness is not the monk who lives in the monastery secluded from people. It is the person who in the midst of crying children, busy schedules, foul-mouthed workers, and rain-soaked days lives a godly life by serving others.

## A Final Thought

Godliness does not come easily. Taking God seriously requires courage, discipline, and persistence. But while godliness may not be an easy life, it is a life of distinction—and other people will take notice. Others notice because the godly person takes on the very imprint of God, reflecting his character. And that reflection is not merely a state of mind; it is manifest in an outpouring of kindness and love.

*Chapter 8*

# BECOMING A MORE LOVING PERSON

. . . and to godliness, brotherly kindness . . .

—2 Peter 1:7

A good character is the best tombstone. Those who loved you, and were helped by you, will remember you when forget-me-nots are withered. Carve your name on hearts, and not on marble.[1]

—Charles Spurgeon

Many years ago there lived two brothers who were farmers, so begins the legend. One lived with his wife and children on one side of a hill, and the other was unmarried and lived in a little hut on the other side of the hill.

One year the brothers each had a particularly good harvest. The married brother stood on his side of the hill, looking at his tall sheaves, and exclaimed, "How good God is! Why does he bless me with more than my brother? I have a wife and children, but my brother is alone. I am so much better off than he is. I do not need all these crops. When my brother is asleep tonight, I shall carry some of my sheaves over the hill to his fields. Tomorrow when he awakens he will never notice what I have done."

While the married brother stood thinking thus, the unmarried brother on the other side of the hill sat in meditation: "God be praised for his loving kindness! But I wish he had done less for me and more for my brother, for my brother has greater needs. I have as much fruit and grain as my brother although my brother must share his harvest with his wife and children. They will share mine too. Tonight, when they are all asleep, I shall place some of my sheaves on my brother's fields. Tomorrow he will never know that he has more or that I have less."

So both brothers waited happily and toward midnight each went to his own fields, loaded his shoulders high with grain, and turned toward the top of the hill. It was exactly midnight when on the summit of the hill the brothers met. Realizing that each had thought only of the other, their hearts overflowed with joy and they warmly embraced one another with tears of happiness.

They lived up to Ralph Waldo Emerson's ideal:

> To leave the world a bit better
>> whether by a healthy child,
>> a redeemed social condition,
>> or a job well done;
> To know even one other life has breathed
>> because you lived—
>> this is to have succeeded.[2]

The apostle Peter instructed us, add to "godliness, brotherly kindness" (2 Peter 1:7). Like the brothers in the legend demonstrated, brotherly kindness is a sincere concern and caring for others. It begins in the family of faith and extends outward as a tangible, pragmatic reflection of Christ's love for the human race. It integrates godliness with a Christlike compassion for others. When we take God seriously we are concerned, caring, and committed to others. Godliness finds its outward expression in loving one another. In fact, godliness is validated by our love for other people.

As will be discussed in the next chapter, the apex of a distinctive life is love. The highest level of Christian maturity is characterized by love. But note, according to Peter's writings, love is built upon brotherly kindness. Both brotherly kindness and love represent the extending of self to others. But each is a distinct trait.

## The Distinction Between Brotherly Kindness and Love

Let's first define brotherly kindness and see how it differs from love. Brotherly kindness is relational—toward one another. It is the act of loving in caring ways toward fellow human beings. It loves because it will get something in return. Love or *agape*, on the other hand, is a love that is awakened by a sense of value in the other. It loves regardless of the response that is reciprocated.

Love always costs the giver. C. S. Lewis wrote, "Love anything, and your heart will certainly be wrung and possibly broken. If you want to make sure of keeping it intact, you must give your heart to no one. . . . It will not be broken: instead, it will become unbreakable, impenetrable, irredeemable."[3] The price of brotherly kindness will generally involve our most prized commodities—time, energy, and money. The cost of *agape* love, however, far outdistances brotherly kindness.

Furthermore, brotherly kindness and love generate different expectations. Brotherly kindness is an act of charity—that is expected—among family and friends. On the other hand, love is an act of charity—that is totally unexpected—toward all people. A thorough study of this unexpected love is presented in the next chapter. For now, attention to the expectations of brotherly kindness follows.

## It Attaches No Strings

Have you ever noticed how strings are often attached to love? First is the "if" string: "I will love you *if* you are good to me"; "I

will love you *if* you change your behavior"; "I will love you *if* you
satisfy my desires." In order to receive this type of love one must
meet certain conditions. Conditional love operates from hidden
agendas and is spurred by selfish motives. It seeks to manipulate
people for its own benefit. Needless to say, conditional love is
strictly superficial.

Another string often attached to love is the "because" string:
"I love you *because* you are pretty"; "I love you *because* you are
rich"; "I love you *because* you give me security." In order to receive this type of love one must possess certain attributes. In other
words, one is loved because of something one is, or something
one does, or something one has. Often this type of love fails to
take into account the needs and concerns of the loved.

Nothing is wrong with loving people for who they are or what
they can do—as long as those attributes are not the sole reason for
love. But if they are, what happens when someone comes along
with better qualities? Or what happens if the beloved loses his or
her qualities? Love dissipates when the attributes no longer exist.

The "if" and "because" strings are attached to love that lacks
sincerity. Inauthentic love seeks to deceive and is self-seeking. It
is not, in fact, love at all. It is a means of controlling another
person, as the following poem reveals.

### The Cold Within

Six humans trapped by happenstance
In bleak and bitter cold.
Each one possessed a stick of wood,
Or so the story's told.

Their dying fire in need of logs,
The first man held his back;
For of the faces 'round the fire,
He noticed one was black.

The next man looking across the way
Saw one not of his church,
And couldn't bring himself to give
The fire his stick of birch.

The third one sat in tattered clothes,
He gave his coat a hitch;
Why should his log be put to use
To warm the idle rich?

The rich man just sat back and thought
Of the wealth he had in store
And how to keep what he had earned
From the lazy, shiftless poor.

The black man's face bespoke revenge
As the fire passed from his sight,
For all he saw in his stick of wood
Was a chance to spite the white.

The last man of this forlorn group
Did naught except for gain.
Giving only to those who gave
Was how he played the game.

Their logs held tight in death's still hands
Was proof of human sin.
They didn't die from the cold without,
They died from the cold within.[4]
        —Author Unknown

Peter instructed us to "have sincere [unhypocritical] love for your brothers, love one another deeply, from the heart" (1 Peter 1:22). Paul exhorted the Romans, "Love must be sincere" (Rom.

12:9). The word *sincere*, found in both verses, comes from the root of the Greek word for *hypocrisy*. In ancient Greece, a hypocrite was a play actor—one who wore masks in dramatic performances in order to deceive the audience. The two scriptural passages cited above, then, exhort that our love be void of hypocrisy. Authentic love never seeks to deceive. It never asks another person to be a "doormat," or a compulsive pleaser, or to maintain peace-at-any-price. Sincere love has no strings attached. It is unconditional. It always accepts and is committed to the growth and happiness of the other person.

## It Commits to Others Like They Are Family

The December 31, 1989, issue of the *Chicago Tribune* featured a series of the best photographs of the decade. Michael Fryer's image captured a fireman and a paramedic carrying a fire victim away from the scene. The blaze Fryer covered seemed routine until firefighters discovered a mother and five children huddled in the kitchen of one apartment. Fryer said firefighters surmised, "She could have escaped with two or three but couldn't decide who to pick, and chose to wait for firefighters to arrive. All of them died of smoke inhalation."

The western view of love is an emotional response, a feeling. But the eastern view of love involves more. It necessitates a commitment for the duration of time. Love is a ten-letter word—commitment. It is one thing to say, "I love you," but quite another to commit yourself to someone for life. The longer one lives the more one realizes that love seems the swiftest, but it is the slowest of all growths. Because it is slow growing we must commit to its development.

The apostle Paul uses an interesting juxtaposition of words in Romans 12:10: "Be devoted to one another in brotherly love." The Greek for *devoted* is a compound word that literally means "love of the family." The word translated *brotherly love* is the familiar Greek word, *philadelphia*. It means literally "love of the brethren." It's intriguing that Paul employs two words—one meaning love of family, the other love of brothers—to communicate the need for commitment in loving. Paul thus exhorts that the deep affection and abiding commitment made between natural family members should be expressed in the spiritual family as well. We are to love our brothers and sisters of faith as we love our brothers and sisters of blood. Brotherly kindness is the affection that family members have for one another.

Furthermore, because God has invited everyone to the family of faith through Christ, every person is a potential brother or sister. Understanding the force of that truth drastically changes the way we respond and treat others. As Christians we are neither isolated individuals nor strangers. We are brothers and sisters in the family of God. Fellow believers may not be in our realm of friends but they are in the scope of our spiritual family. We may not know them by name but we love them as family.

This familial love was one of the most amazing qualities of the early church—and one that the enemies of the church could neither grasp nor understand. In fact, many things about believers puzzled their enemies. One, the enemies thought believers were cannibals. What would you think if you overheard a group of people talking about eating "his" body and drinking "his" blood? Two, the disciples gloried in the cross. The cross was a stumbling block to the Jews and foolishness to the Gentiles. Why? Because the cross was the most dehumanizing form of execution, one that the Roman government reserved for common criminals. Three, nonbelievers could not understand why believers called one another brother and sister. They were not of the same natural family. But as members of the same spiritual family, these people loved and accepted each other. Is it any wonder, then, that the early church increased its membership so rapidly? That people wanted to be a part of a group who accepted them like a natural mother or father would? The enemies of the church nicknamed these disciples "Christians," meaning "little Christs." The dominant feature of Jesus became theirs. Brotherly kindness abounded.

We will never love fellow believers appropriately until we see each other as brothers and sisters. We will not take on the complete character of Christ until we understand that we are part of a family in which love is expected. Jesus has given authority to the entire world to judge whether we are believers or not simply on the basis of our love for one another. "A new command I give you: Love one another. As I have loved you, so you must love one another. By this all men will know that you are my disciples, if you love one another" (John 13:34–35). Love is the badge that identifies us as believers of Jesus Christ. Any time that we do not show love toward fellow believers we forfeit our right to represent Jesus Christ in the world. People around us, who are bored by doctrine and can't fathom theology, do understand love. People look at how Christians act before they look at Christian creed. They form their opinions about our religion when they see how we behave. If they like the melody, they will listen to our words. If what they hear is discord, then the lyrics of our faith seldom register in their lives.

The familiar song "Blest Be the Tie That Binds" reminds us of our call to love:

> Blest be the tie that binds
> Our hearts in Christian love;
> The fellowship of kindred minds
> Is like to that above.
>
> We share each other's woes,
> Each other's burdens bear;
> And often for each other flows
> The sympathizing tear.[5]

As believers in Jesus Christ, committed to exemplifying a distinctive character, we need to make a visible, unequivocal commitment to loving each other as family. Erich Fromm has stated, "To love means to commit oneself without guarantee, to give oneself completely in the hope that our love will produce love in the loved person. Love is an act of faith, and whoever is of little faith is also of little love."[6] Will we commit ourselves to loving others without expecting a guarantee that they will love us in return? Will we love, seeking not love in return but seeking to draw out love in the loved? Will we commit to loving each other as family?

## It Walks a Mile in Another's Moccasins

We can't love at a distance. It has been said that to love is to participate in the life of another. Love happens when we get close enough to our brothers and sisters in Christ so that we can see and understand their needs. Thomas Dubay said, "To care is to jump into the other's skin. It is to become the other in mind and heart, to live the other's interests. To care is to become one's brother, one's sister."[7] America's indigenous peoples said it simply: "I will not judge nor criticize until I have walked a mile in another's moccasins." Love is not merely a feeling. It is an active interest in the well-being of another person. It acts for the benefit of others.

A friend told me the story of a little girl who was sent to her neighbor's house by her mother. When the child returned late, the mother asked, "Why did it take you so long?

The little girl replied, "I saw Annie, and she had dropped her doll and broken it."

The mother asked, "Did you help her fix it?"

"No, Mother, but I sat down and helped her cry."

In modern society the watchword is "Don't get involved," and too often people look the other way so as not to get involved. I read of a newspaper that staged a traffic accident to see how people would respond. A driver rammed a car up over the curb and onto a busy sidewalk, then slumped against the steering wheel, apparently unconscious. For hours no one stopped. Dozens of people walked around the car, ignoring the apparent plight of the driver.

Could it be that God tests the authenticity of our love for him by our demonstration of practical caring for others? Brotherly kindness focuses on other people's needs, hurts, problems, desires, and goals. Following are practical ways we can get involved in another's life:

- *Socially.* "Keep on loving each other as brothers. Do not forget to entertain strangers, for by so doing some people have entertained angels without knowing it" (Heb. 13:1–2). *Entertain strangers* in its original language means "the love of strangers." Thus, not knowing a person is not a license to ignore him or her. Brotherly kindness opens its heart, its hand, and its door. Our homes are to be used of God in loving people, not merely as a showcase for possessions.
- *Emotionally.* We are to spur people on with our optimism, enthusiasm, and encouragement. We all need encouragement, but by the same token, we are all to be encouragers. We need to emotionally lift people on our shoulders, carrying them through the deep waters of suffering and depression. Brotherly kindness does not give up on people.
- *Spiritually.* One of the most loving things a person can do for me is to pray for me. If we love people we will share their concerns with God. Praying for people will not only change them, but it will also change us.
- *Physically.* Our compassion is demonstrated by discovering the needs of other people and then seeking to meet those needs. Loving people means getting our hands dirty, and we can't wait for opportunities—we must find them. Loving people is rarely easy, especially loving the unlovely.

- *Financially.* Brotherly kindness is generous. Many people are intent on getting, but the heart of a believer in Christ desires to give. Hence, love never feels threatened, because it isn't trying to get; it is always trying to give. The Christian community is responsible for meeting the needs of fellow believers. A remarkable feature of the early church was that, even though no one was rich, no one in a congregation starved or lived in poverty. Believers shared all things in common, meeting the needs of the brethren.

What keeps us from involvement? Have we allowed our concerns for major social issues—race, nuclear war, pollution, and abortion—to become an excuse for neglecting our wounded neighbors? Or do we allow good works and activities—church committee meetings or volunteer charity work—to substitute for concerned participation in the lives of others? While social issues and volunteer activities are important for the Christian, let's not use them as an excuse for avoiding personal involvement.

Ted Engstrom accurately identifies the problem and reminds us of our responsibility.

Now, however, we've become adept at organizing, lobbying, propagandizing, and making our collective wills known on the grand issues. We've acquired more expertise in mass persuasion than in individual impact. Why? Perhaps because it's easier to carry a placard to city hall than a casserole next door. It's less threatening to urge a faraway tyrant to release his people than to invite a friend to unburden his soul. The former can serve as a convenient excuse to neglect the latter. The truly caring person begins with those he can eyeball and then extends his influence as far as his gifts and resources will allow.[8]

## It Refuses to Keep Score

The beautiful chapter on love in 1 Corinthians contains a line that many of us would rather not read: Love "keeps no record of wrongs" (13:5). The word *record* in the original Greek was an accounting term that referred to entering an item into a ledger so that it would not be forgotten. It is sad that some people record in their mental account books every pain and injustice they may have experienced. But brotherly kindness refuses to keep score, deciding instead to abandon the impulse to get even. Since God wiped our slates clean, then why can't we do the same for others?

Brotherly kindness forgives those who hurt us. The apostle Paul reminds us, "Forgive whatever grievances you may have against one another. Forgive as the Lord forgave you" (Col. 3:13). One can't love fully and at the same time harbor resentment. Those who hurt us are usually people we are closest to—parents, siblings, spouses, friends, and Christian brothers and sisters. Thus, getting even only leads to a vicious cycle of retaliation. In the long run, forgiveness, like the apostle Paul encourages, is the best choice for the aggrieved and the aggriever. Forgiveness is one of the untapped—and least understood—sources of healing power. Genuine forgiveness is a positive act, one that requires enormous spiritual strength.

When Sue Kidd worked as a nurse, a patient, Mr. Williams, had a slight heart attack. He asked Sue to call his daughter, the only family he had, and tell her that he had had a heart attack. "Of course I'll call her," Sue assured him. Before Sue went to the nurse's station to make the call, Mr. Williams asked for a paper and pencil. She found a scrap of yellow paper and a pen, and handed them to Mr. Williams. Then she went to make the call.

"Janie, this is Sue Kidd, a registered nurse at the hospital. I'm calling about your father. He was admitted tonight with a slight heart attack and—"

"No!" Janie screamed. "He's not dying, is he? You must not let him die!"

"He is getting the very best care."

"But you don't understand," she pleaded. "My daddy and I haven't spoken in almost a year. We had a terrible argument on my twenty-first birthday—over my boyfriend. I ran out of the house. I . . . I haven't been back. All these months I've wanted to go to him for forgiveness. The last thing I said to him was, 'I hate you.'"

Janie said she would be at the hospital in thirty minutes. Before she arrived Mr. Williams went into cardiac arrest. The doctors and nurses could not revive him.

When Sue left Mr. Williams's room she saw Janie leaning against the wall. A doctor had reported to her the sad news. Sue tried to console Janie, knowing her words were pitifully inadequate. "I never hated him, you know," Janie said. "I loved him." Then she whirled toward Sue. "I want to see him."

Janie crept into the room, leaned over the bed, and buried her head in the sheets.

Sue tried not to look at this final, private good-bye. She backed up, and her hand fell upon a scrap of yellow paper. She picked it up and read it.

> My dearest Janie, I forgive you. I pray you will also forgive me. I know that you love me. I love you, too.
>
>                                             Daddy

The note shook in Sue's hands as she thrust it toward Janie. She read it once. Then twice. Her tormented face grew radiant. Peace glistened in her eyes.[9]

That is a picture of the healing power of forgiveness. Life is fragile. Relationships are fragile, too. But they can be mended by the power of forgiveness.

Consider for a moment. This book is about character—distinctive character. You probably haven't attained perfection (or you wouldn't be reading it). Well, neither have I. And if God is patient with us, shouldn't we be patient with others? If God believes our characters can change, then can't we believe that about others? People change, characters do alter. We, therefore, must live in the present and not in the past. At some point we all have been hurt or abused by people we've loved. But if we dwell on the past and the misdeeds of the past then our relationships are doomed. As Alan Loy McGinnis said, "Keeping close books on how many wrongs have been done us makes us become accusatory, for most of us have a short memory for our own mistakes."[10]

It was said of Abraham Lincoln, "He never forgot a kindness and never remembered a wrong." We will entertain an early death by holding grudges and brooding over wrongs. A powerful therapeutic principle for a happy and long life is to forgive and to forget.

"I'll forgive . . . but I'll never forget." We say that and hear it so much, we think it's natural. But failure to forgive and forget leads to inner pain and torment. Will you forgive the ones who have wronged you? Or will you allow bitterness to fester and grow into a cancer that will eventually destroy you?

Consider, too, that failure to forgive and forget is hypocritical. We are to forgive as we have been forgiven. Once General Oglethorpe said to John Wesley, "I never forgive." John Wesley, who was a friend of the general, replied, "In that case, I hope you never sin."

Can you work toward ". . . forgiving each other, just as in Christ God forgave you" (Eph. 4:32)? The greatest debt you owe is to the God of heaven. God's records show that each of you deserve eternal damnation, but he forgives you and pays your debt. If he can forgive and forget, then why can't you?

## It Melts People with Kindness

Henry Drummond's book *The Greatest Thing in the World* is a classic on love. Its pages are filled with powerful instructions on how to dispense love. He writes, "The greatest thing a man can do for his Heavenly Father is to be kind to some of his other children." On another occasion he states, "I shall pass through this world but once. Any good thing, therefore, that I can do, or any kindness that I can show to any human being, let me do it now. Let me not defer it or neglect it, for I shall not pass this way again."[11]

An often misunderstood verse in Scripture is Romans 12:20. The passage begins, "If your enemy is hungry, feed him; if he is thirsty, give him something to drink." In this verse Paul gives us examples of kindness, and in other passages he makes it clear that we are not to be vengeful. An enemy is not one whom we hate, but one who may have bitterness toward us and is unconscious of the barrier that bitterness has created. Often, the one harboring the bitterness is unwilling or unable to scale the wall in order to seek reconciliation. Paul wants us to express kindness toward these people, instructing us to feed our hungry enemy and give a drink to our thirsty enemy. Those are acts of kindness.

Then Paul adds a rather odd statement. In these expressions of kindness "you will heap burning coals on his head." Heaping burning coals on the head of one's enemy is a strange way of showing kindness. And at first reading it sounds like Paul is endorsing the practice of kindness for the purpose of vindictiveness. What does Paul mean? First-century housewives kept a fire going in their ovens at all times. But once a fire went out, it was extremely difficult to start the fire again. When the fire went out, the housewife walked to a neighbor's house and borrowed some red-hot coals. Normally, a woman carried these coals in a container on top of her head. So lending coals with which to start a fire was an expression of kindness. In the Romans passage above, then, Paul is saying that when your neighbor needs hot coals, even if your neighbor is an enemy, you should give your neighbor the coals.

Didn't Jesus suggest the same thing? "If you love those who love you, what credit is that to you? Even 'sinners' love those who love them. . . . But love your enemies, do good to them, and lend to them without expecting to get anything back. Then your reward will be great, and you will be sons of the Most High, because he is kind to the ungrateful and wicked" (Luke 6:32, 35). We can easily love those who love us in return. And loving those who are kind to us is not difficult either. But expressing love and kindness to our enemy is tough. But when we do—did you notice what Jesus said of those who did?—we will be sons of the Most High. We will bear the likeness and the character of Jesus Christ.

The most convincing evidence for brotherly kindness is—at the risk of being redundant—kindness. Kindness is the active expression of love, an affection that never wavers. The kind person is sensitive to the needs of others. He or she has a desire for the happiness of others and turns that desire into action to advance that happiness. William Wordsworth wrote,

> On that best portion of a good man's life,
> His little, nameless, unremembered, acts
> Of kindness and of love.[12]

For what will your life be remembered?

Our names may never appear in the headlines for performing heroic deeds, but we can be kind one to another. We may not travel as an evangelist winning thousands to Christ, but we can express kindness to brothers and sisters, and to those who harbor resentment against us. The expression of kindness seems to be missing from many people's lives—may it not be absent in ours. "What does the Lord require of you[?]" the prophet Micah asks. His answer to his own question includes "to love kindness" (Mic. 6:8 NASB).

The test of our characters is not our religious activity—it is our love. Our love—be it an act of kindness, a forgiving gesture, or helping a brother or sister in need—will not go unnoticed. No expression of compassion to another human being is wasted effort.

A new volunteer had gone to serve with Mother Teresa among the poorest of the poor in Calcutta. On their tour of a children's home, Mother Teresa spotted an infant who had been rescued from the streets, but who was beyond medical help. The child was surely going to die that day.

Mother Teresa picked up the baby and handed her to the new volunteer, with these simple instructions: "Don't let this child die without being loved."

The volunteer later said, "I held her in my arms, and I loved her until she died at six o'clock in the evening. I spent the hours humming Brahms' Lullaby, and do you know—*I could feel that baby, as tiny and as weak as she was, pressing herself against me.*"[13]

Even a dying infant responds to a simple act of brotherly kindness.

*Chapter 9*

# EMULATING GOD'S LOVE

. . . and to brotherly kindness, love.
—2 Peter 1:7

Undaunted radiance is not built on anything passing,
but on the love of God that nothing can alter.[1]
—Oswald Chambers

Love marks the Christian. Love sets the believer apart, distinguishing his or her character. Love is the apex of godly maturity, the ultimate destination in the journey of the believer. It has been said that if there is love in the heart, there will be beauty in the character.

## The Beauty of Love

Peter exhorts us to add "to brotherly kindness, love" (2 Peter 1:7)—the final virtue of distinctive character. The word Peter uses for love is a beautiful word—*agape*.

Greek is an intricate language. Four different words are employed to express the one English word *love*. The word used primarily to express love of family is *storge*. *Philia* expresses deep and warm affection for another. *Eros* refers to physical or sexual love. The fourth word is *agape*.

Following the death and resurrection of Jesus, the Christian

153

writers needed a word to communicate God's unconditional love for people. This idea was wrapped up in *agape,* which became the standard by which Christians were to love friend and enemy alike. *Agape* characterized God's love for humankind and distinguished Christian love from that of the rest of society. It was a one-of-a-kind love that won the hearts of many people to the Christian faith.

What makes *agape* love so appealing?

*Agape* is unlimited. Love that the world knows often boxes people in. If one will enter a box—meet certain conditions, hold similar values and beliefs—one will be loved. Such love is shallow and confining. But *agape* cannot be contained and spills over the lid. It is broad as the heavens, deep as the oceans. It knows no boundaries, creates no conditions, demands no prerequisites. It is demonstrated and expressed, no matter what.

Furthermore, *agape* involves a deliberate choice. *Agape* moves beyond emotion and feelings to become an act of the will. You've heard of premeditated murder, the deliberate and conscious act of killing. *Agape* involves the same premeditated choice and execution, but it results in loving others like God loves us. Regardless of what the loved one does or says, the person practicing *agape* chooses to love. Just like God. Remember, God doesn't love us because we are loveable; he loves us because he has chosen to love us.

Also, *agape* values. *Storge* (familial love) has its basis in one's own nature. *Eros* (romantic love) has its basis in passion. *Philia* (friendly affection) has its basis in pleasurableness. But according to Greek scholar Kenneth Wuest, *agape* is "a love that has its basis in preciousness, a love called out of one's heart by an awakened sense of value in the object loved that causes one to prize it."[2] *Agape* looks beyond the exterior and sees an individual who matters so much to God that he died for that person.

But the most distinguishing quality of *agape* is that it is unexpected. The previous chapter identified brotherly kindness as love that is expected among friends and family of the faith. *Agape* is love that is unexpected, and is demonstrated toward all people—friend and enemy alike. This type of love transcends human reasoning. It embodies the one standard that truly separates the believer from the nonbeliever. Dwight Small wrote,

> Agape is not born of a lover's need, nor does it have its source in the love's object. Agape doesn't exist in order to get what it wants but empties itself to give what the other needs. Its motives rise wholly from within its own nature. Agape lives in order to die to self for the blessedness of caring for another, spending for another, spending itself for the sake of the beloved.[3]

Unexpected love is divine love. It resembles the love God has for all humankind. The Lord tells his people, "I have loved you with an everlasting love; I have drawn you with loving-kindness" (Jer. 31:3). God's love for us defies human understanding. His love is infinite, having no limitations or boundaries. Thus we will never be able to get out of it, or away from it, or beyond it.

And because we are loved, we can love. God's intention—having rescued us from sin and having impressed his nature on us—is to develop a people who reflect his character of love. We are God's "advertisement" of love, what a society and culture could be and how individuals could live in that society. Producing such an advertisement is a long and laborious process, and occurs as believers obey God's command to love as he has loved us. But throughout the process God has committed himself to us, a commitment based on his character, not on our needs or desires. He promises to shine through us as we radiate his character. The highest expression of his character is this unexpected love—*agape*—love for others as God loves us.

## Unexpected Love

Jesus, in his Sermon on the Mount recorded in Matthew 5 through 8, taught the assembled group radical principles about how to live. The theme of this grand sermon was "be different." For each principle, Jesus stated the way the religious types of the day conducted themselves, and then he instructed his followers to be unique. Six times in Matthew 5 alone, Jesus said, "You have heard that it was said . . . But I tell you . . ." In Matthew 5:38–48 Jesus describes a distinctive kind of love. He stated the oldest law in the world, *Lex Talionis,* an eye for an eye and a tooth for a tooth. It was a common practice and a part of everyday life, stained with the blood of vengeance. Jesus now sought to abolish that law with a love so radical that it was totally unexpected. To get his message across he described three scenarios.

The first, "If someone strikes you on the right cheek, turn to him the other also" (Matt. 5:39), creates an unexpected strategy. Suppose you're standing with a group of people, discussing the local Jerusalem archery team. The win–loss record reveals that the team hasn't done well this year. Having been a pretty good marksman in your day, someone asks your opinion for improvement. You enthusiastically offer several suggestions that you think would improve the performance of the team. None are derogatory but most of the suggestions are aimed at the coach. Unbeknownst to you, the coach is on the outskirts of the group. Suddenly a red-faced man steps in front of you and, without any warning, strikes you across the face with the back of his hand.

According to the law and culture of the day, to hit a person with the back of the hand was considered the ultimate humiliation. There you stand, publicly insulted. You feel the swelling of your cheek and you taste your own blood. Your adrenaline is flowing, and your anger is mounting. Your honor is, after all, at stake. You know you can make mince meat out of this bozo.

The group has become strangely silent. What are you going to do? How will you respond? Jesus commanded his followers to turn the other cheek. For you, that means, *Don't slap him back. Don't kick him in the shins. Don't scream at him. Don't curse him or mutter obscenities under your breath.* Instead, you remind yourself that this man is a child of God. You want to retaliate but God has something better planned. Reach for the pinnacle of your character and love this man.

Turning the other cheek is not an act of surrender. It is an unexpected strategy, a positive initiative in loving even those who insult, misunderstand, resent, and even harm you. An action so unexpected will undoubtedly have a profound impact on the offender's life.

Bruce Larson describes an incident that occurred when he was waiting for a bus in New York. Just as he got to the head of the line, a hard-faced, middle-aged woman came from the side and shoved in front of him by planting her elbow in his stomach. Removing the woman's elbow from his stomach, he said, with elaborate sarcasm, "Forgive me. I didn't mean to shove you."

She turned and looked him straight in the eye. "I don't understand it," she said with apology and shock. "Why are you so nice to me? I was really rude—I shouldn't have shoved in line like that."

The woman had reacted to his counterfeit display of love as if it were real. And, for the moment, at least, she was transformed.

But her reaction devastated Larson. Later, on the bus headed home, Bruce prayed silently, "Lord, what are you trying to teach me?"

The Lord seemed to say, "Bruce, I have been trying to tell you, and all my people for centuries, that life upon this earth will not be changed by preaching and teaching and committees, but by people giving up their rightful place in line—every kind of line— simply because I gave up my rightful place when I came to be among you. What I ask is that you who profess to believe in me do the same. My strategy of love will always release a chain reaction of changed lives."[4]

What a strategy! What a radical way of relating and dealing with people. What could be more God-like than turning the other cheek?

Jesus' second scenario is of unexpected sacrifice. "And if someone wants to sue you and take your tunic, let him have your cloak as well" (Matt. 5:40). In ancient times, the tunic, or shirt, was a long inner garment made of cotton or linen. Even the poorest man would have a change of tunics. The cloak, or coat, was a blanket-like outer garment worn as a robe by day and used as a blanket by night. The Jews would probably have only one of these garments.

In the bartering and trading of this time, men would often provide their tunics as collateral until the business deal was finalized. But they would never give up their cloaks. During the cold Palestinian nights, to be without a cloak could be fatal. Furthermore, the cloaks were protected by Jewish law.

Suppose a stonemason purchases some stone from the local stone quarry to make mangers for a sheepherder. The stonemason agrees to pay off the stone in installments over two months. Money is tighter than he anticipates, and he is unable to make his final installment. The owner of the quarry comes for the collateral, the tunic. In light of Jesus' command the stonemason goes a step further. He gives the quarry owner not only his tunic, but his cloak as well. He says, "I want to be known as a trustworthy trader. I haven't fulfilled my obligation of the bargain. I know that the cloak is protected by law, but I still want you to have it. I can get by without it until I pay off the debt. I want to show you and all men of trade that I am a man of my word."

Giving up the cloak is not merely a wise business ploy, but an unexpected sacrifice in action. The act moves beyond law-keeping and rights. This radical love is willing to surrender what rightfully belongs to the giver. At great expense to the giver, the one who receives enters a place of honor and esteem. The receiver's rights are given priority over those of the giver's. In fact, unexpected sacrifice underlies all of Jesus' teachings concerning love. The greater the sacrifice the greater the love.

Martin Luther King Jr. and other leaders of the Civil Rights movement of the 1960s demonstrated unexpected sacrifice. Read King's words. They ring with sacrifice and the anticipated consequence of such gracious action.

> Do to us what you will and we will still love you. . . . Throw us in jail and we will still love you. Bomb our homes and threaten our children, and, as difficult as it is, we will still love you. Send your hooded perpetrators of violence into our communities at the midnight hour and drag us out on some wayside road and leave us half-dead as you beat us, and we will still love you. . . . But be assured that we'll wear you down by our capacity to suffer, and one day we will win our freedom. We will not only win freedom for ourselves; we will so appeal to your heart and conscience that we shall win you in the process, and our victory will be a double victory.[5]

His words remind me of an incident that happened several years ago. The USS Pueblo, a ship from the United States Navy, was hijacked by the North Korean military. The incident provoked a tense diplomatic and military standoff. The eighty-two surviving crew members suffered through a period of brutal captivity. In one particular instance thirteen of the men were required to sit in a rigid manner around a table for hours. After several hours, the door to the room was flung open and a North Korean guard brutally beat the man in the first chair with the butt of his rifle. The next day, as each man sat at his assigned place, again the door was thrown open and the man in the first chair was brutally beaten. On the third day, it happened again to the same man.

Knowing that the man could not survive another beating, the next day another young sailor took his place. When the door was flung open, the guard automatically beat the new victim sense-less. For days, a new man stepped forward each day to sit in that horrible chair, knowing full well what would happen. At last the guards gave up in exasperation. They were unable to overcome that kind of sacrificial love.

The third scenario spoke to one of the most hated practices under Roman rule—impressment. "If someone forces you to go one mile, go with him two miles" (Matt. 5:41). This scenario creates an image of unexpected service. Roman soldiers were sta-tioned throughout all provinces in Palestine, and every Roman soldier had the legal right to approach any civilian and impress him or her into service. Of all the services the Jews were forced to perform, the one most hated was carrying the Roman soldier's baggage. The Jews had apparently voiced such objections and so the Romans placed a limit on the service. A Roman could force a Jew to carry the pack for one mile only.

Envision that you are working in your carpentry shop, and a deadline is upon you. An order for a table and chairs has to go out tomorrow. It is late afternoon as the sun streams through the open door of your workshop. Suddenly, a shadow stretches across the floor. You look up from your workbench, and silhouetted against the afternoon sun is a Roman soldier. You can tell by the outline of his headgear and uniform. He mutters gruffly, "Come, carry my pack." Of all the times to be impressed into service. You want so desperately to finish before nightfall. But the project will have to wait.

Off you go, lugging a pack that weighs you down like a ton of bricks. The Roman soldier meanders behind, snacking on dates. Eventually, you come to the mile marker. (The Jews posted sticks on every road leading out of their villages so they would not have to walk one step beyond what was expected.) How do you respond? Some Jews would slam the bag down, hoping break-able objects of value were in the bag. Others would spit on the ground, demonstrating how they detest their service. Others would curse, kicking up dust returning home. But how does Jesus say to respond? *Go a second mile.* Instead of slamming the pack down you readjust its position and, to the shock and bewilderment of the Roman soldier, you keep on walking. The soldier stands in utter disbelief, thinking *Something is different about this guy. In all of my travels, I have never encountered such loving service.*

Going the second mile is not a sign of weakness. It is an unexpected service of love. True Christian love is never expressed in the first mile. The first mile is expected. That is obligatory, even mandatory. Christian love is always expressed in the second mile, serving beyond what is expected.

A well-known Bible teacher once spoke to a men's group at a church in the Washington, D. C., area. Afterward, he noticed a man who stayed behind to remove and stack the chairs. Upon inquiring, he learned that the man was a United States senator. It did not take any of the talent or ability usually associated with being a senator to stack chairs. But it did take the unexpected attitude of a servant. A serving love is an active love—regardless of one's station in life—that constantly seeks to meet the needs of others.

An amazing power exists in unexpected service. When we exceed the minimums of service, when we go beyond the call of duty, when we give more than is expected, it has a potent and transforming effect on people.

## What Does This Mean to Us?

For centuries people have read these directives from Jesus and tried to make sense of them. What, then, can we learn from them? Following are general applications.

### *Jesus Modeled Unexpected Love*

*Agape* was at the heart of Jesus' life. He was cursed, beaten, slapped, and mocked; nails were driven into his body. He could have aroused the forces of heaven to avenge these horrible injustices. Instead, he turned the other cheek and forgave his tormentors: "Father, forgive them, for they do not know what they are doing" (Luke 23:34).

At the center of Jesus' plan for the salvation of mankind was sacrifice. Without the shedding of blood there is no forgiveness of sin. Jesus was the precious lamb, who was slaughtered on our behalves. His actions throughout his life can be boiled down to one verse: "The Son of Man did not come to be served, but to serve, and to give his life as a ransom for many" (Matt. 20:28). Many did not comprehend his motives then; many do not comprehend his motives now.

Jesus lived loving—unexpected strategy, unexpected sacrifice, unexpected service. He commands us to "love each other as I have loved you" (John 15:12). Jesus chose this role in life, and he calls us to be like him.

## *Unexpected Love Must Be Practiced*

Loving in a radical, unexpected manner is probably the most difficult of challenges. Human nature tends toward getting even and looking out for number one. Loving as Jesus loved is tough. But through consistent practice we can demonstrate *agape* love. We'll have to endure slaps every day—giving up our rightful place in line, being cut off in traffic. We'll need to become less defensive. We'll have to go beyond the call of duty, beyond what is expected. We'll need to sacrifice personal time, rights, and energy for others.

It may take a while to get the hang of it. But those around us will be affected by the simple way we love. Imagine the impact this type of loving will have on those with whom you work— your boss will do a double take when you do more than is required; your associates will question your motives when you serve them. Families will be strengthened—marriages will move out of the rut and grow; children and parents will relate and enjoy each other's company.

## Unexpected Love Contains Healing Powers

Selfless love will have a radical effect on your health and life. David McClelland, Ph.D., of the Harvard Medical School, in an effort to persuade his medical students to use "tender loving care" with their patients, demonstrated the power of love to make the body healthier. Dr. McClelland showed a group of Harvard students a documentary of Mother Teresa ministering with love to the sick. Dr. McClelland measured the levels of immunoglobulin A (IgA) in the students' saliva before and after viewing the film. IgA is an antibody against viral infections such as colds and flu. IgA levels rose significantly in the students who saw the documentary, even in those who were not particularly religious.[6]

Loving others is good for health. Acts of compassion are acts of self-healing. We gain strength by giving strength. It is a grace of God that inherent in his radical plan of loving is our own experience of healing through helping. When we ease the pain of others through service and sacrifice, our own burdens become lighter. Life is no longer meaningless.

## Unexpected Love Has a Profound Effect on Other People

As we have seen in the preceding stories, this radical love affects people, making a deep, lasting impression. Can anything have a more profound effect on the lives of spiritually hardened men and women than unexpected love?

Return to the scene of the cross once again. As Jesus died, a hardened Roman centurion broke down and cried, "Surely he was the Son of God!" (Matt. 27:54). This soldier was broken by the power of Jesus' radical, nonretaliatory, second-mile love.

What Jesus did for the centurion we can do for others. Love may be the most powerful apologetic in the Christian's arsenal. Apologetics is the art of persuading people of the truth of Christianity. When true love is demonstrated, people are changed. Love, hand in hand with truth, is the strongest persuasion any believer can offer to a watching world. When hungering souls see radical, unexpected love in Christians they are drawn irresistibly to the Christian faith. Love is the most powerful message we can preach.

The little church's aisles swelled with the Easter gathering until there were no more pews to squeeze into. The organ and the piano harmonized "He Is Risen" a few extra times while the ushers lined up the last chairs from the church hall along the back of the sanctuary. A few more latecomers edged down the side aisles and leaned against the walls.

Then Andy entered. He beamed with a sense of Easter joy until he saw that "his" spot in the back row was filled. Regular attendees usually left the seat empty, knowing that Andy would arrive late from the home for the learning disabled.

Confusion was evident on his face as the prelude ended and Andy found no place to sit. With characteristic simplicity, Andy made his way up the center aisle. He made his way to a large open space just below the platform where the elders, ministers, and choir members stood poised to open the service. Then he lowered his huge body to the floor, crossing his legs Indian style.

As the rest of the congregation sat down, Marvin, a deacon in the church for many years, left his place in the pew and started up the center aisle toward Andy. It took Marvin a long time to reach the front. Respect for this eighty-year-old servant, much loved by all, or perhaps sheer curiosity brought a hush over the whole church. Even the minister gripped the arms of his chair and watched.

What was Marvin going to do? One could not blame him for asking Andy to move. He was, after all, out of place, and this was a reverent church service. By now all eyes were on the deacon, anticipating that he would ask the young man to get up.

But Marvin did the unexpected. He shifted his lean frame onto his cane and with difficulty lowered his aged body to the floor beside Andy. The two worshiped together that day, sitting Indian style on the plush carpet of a dignified church.

When the minister stood to preach, tears came to his eyes. He closed his Bible over his sermon notes and said, "Our sermon has just been preached."[7]

## Fulfilling Our Purpose

As Jesus spoke to the crowd on the mountainside that day telling them to be different, to love unexpectedly, he likely knew that his audience was shaking their heads, thinking, *But why do we have to love in this manner?* "That you may be sons of your Father in heaven" (Matt. 5:45). The reason is very simple, yet at the same time very powerful; the demonstration of unexpected love makes us children of God.

The Hebrew language does not contain many adjectives, therefore, the language often uses *son of* with an abstract noun, where English would use an adjective. For example, the Hebrew *son of peace* is *peaceful man* in English; a *daughter of consolation* is a *consoling woman*. Hence, a *child of God* is a *godlike person*. The reason we must demonstrate Jesus' unexpected strategy, and unexpected sacrifice, and unexpected service is that God manifested it. And if we express it, we become nothing less than sons and daughters of our heavenly Father, reflecting the very nature of God. We express the radical and distinctive character of love.

Love is the crown of distinctive character. We are never more like God than when we love. I love the statement, "Human love is a reflection of something in the divine nature itself." And what is the dominant aspect of God's nature? Love. Clement of Alexandria described the real Christian as one who practices being God. And what is God? Love. When we give love—unconditionally, unexpectedly, and graciously—to friend and enemy alike, we are like God.

Understanding Jesus' command, "Love your enemies and pray for those who persecute you, that you may be sons of your Father in heaven" (Matt. 5:44–45), illuminates one of the most difficult verses in the New Testament, Matthew 5:48: "Be perfect, therefore, as your heavenly Father is perfect." At face value Jesus' command appears impossible to fulfill. The Greek word for *perfect* is *teleios*. The word does not mean sinless perfection but refers to a person who has reached *teleios*—maturity—as opposed to a child or adolescent. A student who has reached a mature knowledge of his subject is *teleios* as opposed to a novice who has yet to grasp the elementary truths.

Stated another way, the Greek idea of perfection relates to function. An object is perfect if it truly and totally fulfills the purpose for which it was planned, designed, and made. A chair is perfect if it provides one a place to sit. A piano is perfect if it brings forth music. A person is perfect if he or she fulfills the purpose for which he or she was created and sent into this world. And for what purpose were human beings created? God said, "Let us make man in our image, in our likeness" (Gen. 1:26). The apostle Paul said, "For those God foreknew he also predestined to be conformed to the likeness of his Son" (Rom. 8:29). People were created to be like God—and God is love. When we love the saint and sinner alike, we fulfill the purpose of God for our lives.

When Jesus commanded us to be perfect, he spoke not of a goal attainable only in heaven; he provided an objective attainable in this life.

Henry Drummond's magnificent work on love, *The Greatest Thing in the World,* addresses love as the essence of God's character. When you receive one you receive the other; to be possessed by one you are possessed by the other. Drummond's words both challenge and inspire, and provide a fitting conclusion to this chapter.

Let at least the first great object of our lives be to achieve the character . . . of Christ—which is built around love. What makes a man a good man? Practice. Nothing else. There is nothing capricious about religion. We do not get the soul in different ways, under different laws, from those in which we get the body and the mind. If a man does not exercise his arm he develops no biceps muscle; and if a man does not exercise his soul, he acquires no muscle in his soul, no strength of character, no vigor of moral fibre, no beauty of spiritual growth. Love is not a thing of enthusiastic emotion. It is a rich, strong, manly, vigorous expression of the whole round Christian character—the Christlike nature in its fullest development.[8]

PART THREE

# THE SECRET

*For if you possess these qualities in increasing measure,*
*they will keep you from being ineffective and unproductive*
*in your knowledge of our Lord Jesus Christ. But if anyone*
*does not have them, he is nearsighted and blind, and has*
*forgotten that he has been cleansed from his past sins. There-*
*fore, my brothers, be all the more eager to make your call-*
*ing and election sure. For if you do these things, you will*
*never fall, and you will receive a rich welcome into the*
*eternal kingdom of our Lord and Savior Jesus Christ.*

*—2 Peter 1:8–11*

*Chapter 10*

# A Toolbox for the Journey

For if you possess these qualities in increasing measure . . .
—2 Peter 1:8

God will not look you over for medals, degrees or diplomas, but for scars.[1]
—Elbert Hubbard

My friend Fred packs a toolbox along with his other luggage when he takes a trip. I asked, "Fred, why do you take all those tools with you on your trips? They only take up space. Don't they?"

"Well, Rick," Fred replied, "I never know when I might need them, especially on a long deserted stretch of highway. They are packed for my protection and my security. Don't you pack tools in your trunk when you travel?"

"Uh . . . no. But from now on," I assured him, "I'll take along some tools. Just for you, Fred."

"Don't do it just for me, take them along for you. You never know when you might need them."

For any journey a toolbox is essential, even in the quest to develop a distinctive character. The following tools are necessary for your journey.

## Wise Choices

Our characters are affected by the decisions we make every day. The choices we made yesterday affect today. The decisions we make today will impact tomorrow.

Our example for wise decision-making is Jesus. It was prophesied of him that "he knows enough to reject the wrong and choose the right" (Isa. 7:15). At the outset of Jesus' ministry he was led into the wilderness and tempted by Satan. I refer to that experience as the "Three Great Decisions" of Jesus. Satan enticed Jesus with power, greed, and lust. Each time the Devil offered his deal, the Lord Jesus responded with authority: "No!" Jesus' decisions set the stage for his ministry and his life. He was not a puppet tossed to and fro by the waves of sensationalism. He was the King of Kings and Lord of Lords, who set an example for all humankind to follow.

In like manner, character is forged by the daily decisions we make. Paul Harvey made an insightful remark on one of his broadcasts after the untimely death of Mike Todd. Todd was a Hollywood entrepreneur, who was married to Elizabeth Taylor at the time. "No one can decide the length of one's life," said Harvey, "but we do make the decisions that determine its width and its depth."

What decisions must be made? I'm not talking about what college to attend, or whom to marry, or what profession to enter, or when to retire—though these decisions are important. The choices that determine the depth of life are the ones regarding our characters of moral excellence, knowledge, self-control, perseverance, godliness, brotherly kindness, and love. They evince themselves through the wife who remains faithful to her husband, the athlete who refuses to take drugs to improve performance, the student who "cracks the books" rather than buying a term paper on the Internet, the salesman who does not pad his expense account to defray an unexpected cost.

Consider Joseph as described in Genesis 39. He made the decision early in life to serve God. That choice guided his future endeavors. Joseph proved his character over and over again, but never as eloquently as when Potiphar's wife made a play for him. Smitten by Joseph's good looks, she brazenly invited him, "Come to bed with me!" (v. 7). Without hesitation, Joseph refused. His decision had already been established in his heart. He could have rationalized, *I am the servant, and she is the employer.* Instead he answered, "How then could I . . . sin against God?" (v. 9). Joseph's desire to please God was more important than wanton pleasure.

Potiphar's wife, however, would not be put off. Shrewdly, she arranged for the servants to be away. Joseph entered the house. She grabbed his shirt saying, "Come to bed with me!" (v. 12). But he fled, leaving his garment in her hand. Sometimes the only escape from lust is to run away. It was that decision to remain pure that kept his character intact.

The world not only seeks, it often expects moral compromise—from business to sports, from politics to the family. What are we to do? If you are tempted to give in, run away. Quit hanging around the enticement of sin; stop flirting with even the appearance of sin. "Flee the evil desires of youth" (2 Tim. 2:22), commanded the apostle Paul, even if it means quitting a job, a career, or a team. God is more concerned with godly character than with status.

Failure to make an upright decision often results in compromise. Small at first, but one compromise leads to another. The compromise escalates. Compromise leads to sin. Eventually, sin destroys character.

When we make decisions, we should consider not only the immediate effects but the future consequences as well. Many politicians can testify about ghosts in the closet. They all come back to haunt. On the other hand, the reward of good decisions is the continuing influence of God in your life and its resulting impact upon others. Over time, good decisions get good results.

When decisions are made in advance they are more likely to be adhered to. When we wait until the point of encounter with Satan the battle is usually lost. A woman prone to drink, for instance, makes the decision before going to a party not to drink. When she is thrust into a situation where a drink is offered she quickly says *no* without giving it any thought. Furthermore, the decision made in advance will help to assure that precautions are taken to help in times of weakness. In this case, a friend accompanies the partygoer to offer encouragement, and another confidante holds her accountable for her behavior. The temptation is thwarted. Character is strengthened.

## Take a Stand

Like an onion is composed of many layers, our convictions become established by making layers of choices. One cannot be a person of character without deep convictions. A person with convictions knows what he or she believes and why. Convictions are not forced on an individual; they are beliefs and actions of choice. Francis Kelley wrote, "Convictions are the mainsprings of action, the driving powers of life. What a man lives are his convictions."[2] Martin Luther King Jr. often told his children, "If a man hasn't discovered something that he will die for, he isn't fit to live."[3]

What are we willing to die for? What convictions should we possess? Convictions must rest on the knowledge of truth as spelled out in Scripture. "My people are destroyed from lack of knowledge" (Hos. 4:6). Jesus said, "Whoever has my commands and obeys them, he is the one who loves me" (John 14:21). Ignorance, whatever its cause, is the reason many people have no convictions. The knowledge needed to mold our convictions comes from being intimately acquainted with God's Word. Without it we wither like grass in the heat of temptation. Conviction-less people do whatever they feel.

The story of Daniel and his three friends is recorded in Daniel 3. These four young men were different; they knew exactly what God wanted them to do and not to do. They had carefully studied the Law of Moses and had gained, by faith, deep convictions on how they should live in the midst of a heathen people. They could stand strong, even when they found themselves completely alone, because of these deep-rooted convictions.

Because they refused to fall down and worship the golden image of Nebuchadnezzar, Daniel's three friends faced execution in the fiery furnace. They were utterly convinced that they must, in complete obedience, do what God's law said, whatever the consequences. Thus, in response to the king's demand to worship the golden image the three men answered, "If we are thrown into the blazing furnace, the God we serve is able to save us from it, and he will rescue us from your hand, O king. But even if he does not, we want you to know, O king, that we will not serve your gods or worship the image of gold you have set up" (Dan. 3:17–18).

How would you have responded? Would you have rationalized or justified falling down to this heathen image? Would you have compromised your beliefs, your convictions? Or would you have stood tall and pronounced boldly as did the three Jews, "No way, King Nebuchadnezzar, we will serve only the Lord God. He will protect us. Even if he doesn't we will gladly die for his sake."

Watching the movie *Chariots of Fire*,[4] I was inspired by Eric Liddell's conviction not to run on Sunday, a conviction forged out of a strong belief in the biblical law of "remember[ing] the Sabbath day by keeping it holy" (Exod. 20:8). He had trained for a single track event, but honoring his convictions meant dashing his hopes of winning an Olympic medal. But his desire and hope did not end in splinters. He entered another event, one for which he had not prepared. Victory seemed impossible. Then, just before the race, one of the contestants put a note in Eric's hand: "He who honors Me, I will honor." Eric ran in faith. His convictions were uncompromised. He honored God, and God honored him. Eric Liddell won the gold medal.

In the quest for character, convictions are prerequisite. Know what you believe. Determine what you will stand for, and if called upon, what you will die for.

## The Writings on the Pages of Life

I believe it was Thomas Carlyle who wrote, "Conviction is worthless unless it is converted into conduct." When one makes choices, those decisions, taken together, establish convictions. And when one lives out one's convictions, the resulting conduct produces character. Solomon wrote, "The character of even a child can be known by the way he acts—whether what he does is pure and right" (Prov. 20:11 LB). "A man is known by his actions. An evil man lives an evil life; a good man lives a godly life" (21:8 LB).

The relationship between character and conduct is so intimate that the two cannot be separated. In fact, they feed each other. True, character is who we are, but character is a process that begins with being and leads to doing. Thus, a cycle is created— what we are, we do; what we do, we become. Character determines conduct, and conduct produces character. Therefore, it is important that we practice godly conduct each day, for in the end we become what we do.

Madame Chiang Kai-Shek was the First Lady of China during World War II. She was an inspiration to the Chinese in their struggle against the Japanese. In one of her radio speeches she said,

> If the past has taught us anything it is that every cause brings its effect, every action has a consequence. We Chinese have a saying: "If a man plants melons he will reap melons; if he sows beans, he will reap beans." And this is true of everyone's life; good begets good, and evil leads to evil.

True enough, the sun shines on the saint and the sinner alike, and too often it seems that the wicked prosper. But we can say with certainty that, with the individual as with the nation, the flourishing of the wicked is an illusion, for, unceasingly, life keeps books on us all.

In the end, we are all the sum total of our actions. Character cannot be counterfeited, nor can it be put on and cast off as if it were a garment to meet the whim of the moment. Like the markings on wood which are ingrained in the very heart of the tree, character requires time and nurturing for growth and development.

Thus also, day by day, we write our own destiny; for inexorably . . . we become what we do.[5]

Madame Chiang Kai-Shek's words are poignant and true. They touch our hearts, causing each of us to ask, "What kind of destiny am I writing on the pages of my life?"

Suppose you were a television reporter assigned to do a story on you. You, the reporter, will cover you, the person, from morning till night. What will the reporter discover at the office, the gym, the kitchen, the television set? What will the camera photograph when no one is looking? What will the tape recorder capture as you talk with and about other people? Will it reveal the nature of God's love and kindness? Our lives, privately and publicly, reveal the markings of character.

The worst and the best of a country is recorded in 2 Chronicles 33 and 34. The chronicler says of Manasseh and Amon, two of the worst kings of Judah, "Manasseh led Judah and the people of Jerusalem astray, so that they did more evil than the nations the Lord had destroyed before the Israelites" (33:9); Amon "did evil in the eyes of the Lord, as his father Manasseh had done" (v. 22).

When Amon died, his son Josiah became king. And because Josiah had a heart for God, when he strode into the darkness that shrouded Judah, a light began to flicker. It eventually glowed, casting its beam throughout the nation. At age sixteen he began to seek God fervently and earnestly. At twenty, he began to purge Judah of the false gods and idols. By the time Josiah reached twenty-six all of Judah was, at least outwardly, cleansed of idolatrous practices. A nation was transformed in six years.

A deeper problem, however, remained—a spiritual problem. Outwardly the nation was cleansed of its unrighteousness. One can enact law, but one cannot legislate righteousness.

When Josiah was twenty-six, a discovery was made during the cleaning and restoration of the temple. A book of the law, lost for eighty years, was found. Josiah read and studied it. The contents of this book had a profound effect on his life. For eighty years no one had read the book, no one had believed the book, and no one had followed the book.

Josiah immediately took action. He gathered the leaders of Judah together and read the book to them. He then made a promise to God. Things would change. First, Josiah consciously decided to do "what was right in the eyes of the LORD" (2 Chron. 34:2). Then following the reading of the book a conviction was solidified: "The king stood by his pillar and renewed the covenant in the presence of the LORD—to follow the LORD and keep his commands, regulations and decrees with all his heart and all his soul, and to obey the words of the covenant written in this book" (v. 31).

His conviction was converted into action.

> Then he had everyone in Jerusalem and Benjamin pledge themselves to it; the people of Jerusalem did this in accordance with the covenant of God, the God of their fathers. Josiah removed all the detestable idols from all the territory belonging to the Israelites, and he had all who were present in Israel serve the LORD their God. As long as he lived, they did not fail to follow the LORD, the God of their fathers. (vv. 32–33)

A single man, Josiah, changed the course of a nation's history. He made a difference in his world. People responded, even marveled. And God was pleased.

## The Consistency Key

Character is born out of conduct that is consistent. Conduct repeated—over and over—yields character. As the poet Charles Reade wrote,

> Sow an act, and you reap a habit.
> Sow a habit, and you reap a character.
> Sow a character, and you reap a destiny.[6]

Plutarch defined character as "simply a long habit continued."

In contrast to a world of fast-food restaurants, jiffy oil changes, instant Internet access, and overnight successes, a character of godliness and love doesn't come so quickly. Character requires consistent behavior.

Who we are when no one is looking should be the same as when people are looking. Just as a coin has two sides to make it authentic and genuine, we have two sides—a private side and a public side. A harmonious relationship between the sides must exist for us to be authentic and genuine. We may fake, fraud, and counterfeit character for a season, but eventually consistency—or rather the lack thereof—will reveal our true natures.

The apostle Paul wrote, "Do not be deceived: God cannot be mocked. A man reaps what he sows" (Gal. 6:7). The author Oscar Wilde knew that in the end we pay for our inconsistencies. William Barclay quotes Wilde's confession:

> The gods had given me almost everything. But I let myself be lured into long spells of senseless and sensual ease.
> . . . Tired of being on the heights, I deliberately went to

the depths in search for new sensation. What the para-
dox was to me in the sphere of thought, perversity became to me in the sphere of passion. I grew careless of
the lives of others. I took pleasure where it pleased me,
and passed on. I forgot that every little action of the common day makes or unmakes character, and that therefore what one has done in the secret chamber, one has
some day to cry aloud from the house-top. I ceased to be
lord over myself. I was no longer the captain of my soul,
and did not know it. I allowed pleasure to dominate me.
I ended in horrible disgrace.[7]

The truth of Wilde's confession is that nothing goes unnoticed. Everything that goes around comes around. Or in his words
"what one has done in the secret chamber, one has some day to
cry aloud from the house-top." Truly we reap what we sow. If we
choose consistency the eventual fruit is character. If we choose
inconsistency a mediocre, if not horrible, existence is our reward.

Consistency is where performance links with stated aims.
Choices are in harmony with convictions. Convictions agree with
conduct. Conduct is repeated until a life of distinctive character
consistently dominates.

## Thinning the Ranks

Our desire is for more than the production of a good, moral,
upstanding citizen; or one who is devoted to one's spouse; or
one who is truthful and honest in business dealings; or one who
is sincere in one's daily walk. Granted all of these and more will
be present when character emerges. But the quest is for building
a distinctive character. A human life that resembles the divine
life. A nature of love in the midst of unloveliness. In order for
that brand of life to emerge a devotion to God must be present.

The writer of Proverbs said it well: "If you want favor with both God and man, and a reputation for good judgment and common sense, then trust the Lord completely; don't ever trust yourself. In everything you do, put God first, and he will direct you and crown your efforts with success" (Prov. 3:4–6 LB).

Commitment is the one ingredient that spells the difference between shallow living and experiencing the depths of a meaningful life—a life that is pleasing and honoring to God. When it comes to character, many people are content with the status quo, mediocrity, and conformity. "The Christian leader," Ted Engstrom writes, "never equates mediocrity with the things of God."[8] I offer an encouraging word, an attainable goal, but most of all a challenge: Godly character can be yours if you make a commitment to develop it.

But be warned—the call to commitment thins the ranks. Jesus makes tough demands. At one point in his ministry many followed Jesus because of curiosity rather than commitment. Knowing this, he turned to the crowd and said, "Unless you eat the flesh of the Son of Man and drink his blood, you have no life in you" (John 6:53). Jesus meant, "If you want to follow me you must take all of me, not just the free meals [the feeding of the 5,000 had just occurred] and the miracles [Jesus walking on the water was fresh on their minds]." As a result, "On hearing it, many of his disciples said, 'This is a hard teaching. Who can accept it?' . . . From this time many of his disciples turned back and no longer followed him" (John 6:60, 66). From the outset of Jesus' ministry he demanded one's all.

Why do twenty-first century Christians think he would want less today?

Woven through the fabric of character are the threads of commitment. The price of distinctive character is abandonment to Jesus Christ. When you do that, you stand apart from the crowd, living a life of distinctive character.

*Chapter 11*

# A LIFETIME WORK

For this reason make every effort. . . .
—2 Peter 1:5

Character cannot be developed through good resolutions and checklists. It usually requires a lot of hard work, a little pain and years of faithfulness before any of the virtues are consistently noticeable in us.[1]
—Bill Hybels

A minister, nearing retirement, purchased a small abandoned farm outside town. The house was in dire need of maintenance. The windows were broken. The paint had peeled from the scorching summer sun. The roof leaked. The floor of the porch gaped with holes.

Three acres accompanied the farm. Its land had not been used for farming in many years. Weeds choked the fields. Debris and litter dotted the landscape. A few fence posts remained but no wire or boards connected them.

The minister had high hopes for the property. Contrary to many well-wishers and advisors, he knew the place was not only livable but could be attractive and self-supporting. He was counting on retiring to this place.

On his weekly day off the minister worked on the farm. He was diligent. He did a little here, a little there. During the cold winter months he worked inside—replacing the plumbing, re-wiring the electricity, painting and wallpapering. When the weather warmed he worked outside. He repaired the roof, re-placed the windows, built new porches, painted, put up shut-ters, erected a white picket fence. He cleared the land, cut the weeds, and turned the soil. He planted a garden with vegetables and flowers.

In an amazingly short period of time, this dilapidated farm became a showpiece. Friends and townspeople were impressed with the minister's work. Several people made offers to purchase the cottage and farm.

One day the minister's neighbor from town came to visit the country cottage. The city-dweller gawked at the garden growing out back, the newly restored house and barn, and the beautiful landscape of the farm. He said, "You and the Lord really did a marvelous work here!"

The minister looked up from his workbench, where he was building garden benches. He wiped the perspiration from his eyes and thought for a moment. He then replied, "Yeah, but you should have seen it when the Lord had it all to himself."[2]

The quest for distinctive character requires hard work and con-sistent effort. True, God shares his being with every believer. But the believer is to work diligently at the task of conforming his or her life to God's nature. Just as it took two—God and a dedi-cated worker—to transform a run-down farm into a beautiful home, it will take two—God and a diligent believer—to trans-form a character from mediocrity to magnificence. God has done his part by imprinting his nature in us. Now we must do our part by working on that impression, adding the virtues of goodness, knowledge, self-control, perseverance, godliness, brotherly kind-ness, and love.

There are no shortcuts to adding these virtues. Peter informed his readers that they "may participate in the divine nature" of God (2 Peter 1:4). In the next verse he instructed, "For this reason, make every effort to add to your faith . . ." (v. 5). *Make every effort* is sometimes translated "diligence." Diligence may lack glamour, but it is the only way to honor God's high calling. *Make every effort* means literally "to make haste," "to be eager," "to do one's best," or "to exert one's self." Make no mistake, a major prerequisite for maturity in Christ is giving the job everything we've got. Consistent effort and hard work are essential.

Daily we engage in a spiritual workout, exercising and developing the character God has entrusted to us and impressed on us. When we physically work out, the tone of our muscles reflect it; likewise, when we spiritually exercise, the tone of our character reflects it. As we do our parts, what began as a choice for morality in an immoral world ends with a love that is so unexpected that people marvel as they notice a life of distinctive character.

J. R. Miller, writing in *The Building of Character*, said, "No magnificent building ever grew up by a miracle. Stone by stone it rose, each block laid in its place by toil and effort. You cannot dream yourself into character, you must hammer and forge yourself into one."[3] The thrust of biblical teaching emphasizes the long-term, patient, undramatic building of Christian character through undramatic means—inch by inch . . . stone by stone . . . step by step. I have not yet arrived at this distinctive character, but I am still pursuing the goal. Daily I am challenged in the areas of morality and self-control. At other times I struggle to love people as God has loved me. I still strain and stretch toward a distinguished life.

The difference between a good work and a great work is in the details. A story has it that Michelangelo worked painstakingly on one part of the Sistine Chapel that would not be seen by the general public. An associate asked, "Why are you going to such great trouble in that place when no one will see it?" Michelangelo replied simply, "I will." And I might add, "God will."

We must give strict attention to every detail of character, from moral excellence to love. Usually those areas that gain public notice are given highest priority, but we must give equal attention to the private sectors of our lives. The virtues that Peter laid out for the formation of a distinctive character are, for the most part, the work of the heart. They require effort in the private domain. It has been said that character is who we are in the dark. Thus, the virtues Peter listed are developed when no one is looking. Eventually who we are in the private domain seeps into the public arena.

Remember that God always works from the perspective of eternity. When God wants to grow an oak tree he takes one hundred years; when he wants to make a squash he takes six weeks. What do you want to be? An oak tree or a squash? Urgency is not utmost. So rather than succumb to the tyranny of the urgent, let us strive for the triumph of character.

It has been said that the highest reward for a man's toil is not what he gets for it, but rather what he becomes by it. When we are diligent at the work of shaping our characters in accordance to God's plan, the benefits are life changing. We become more and more like our Creator.

The tasks before you are not easy. At times they will be difficult and hard pressing. You may even want to succumb to the world, forgo self-control, beg to give up, hate instead of love. But stay on the course, though tempted to look for shortcuts. There are none.

The ultimate result, however, is worth the effort. In the end, God—if not the world—will take notice of your life and of your distinctive character.

# Notes

## Introduction

1. Cited in Stephen Donadio, ed., *The New York Public Library Book of Twentieth-Century American Quotations* (New York: Warner Books, 1992), 242.
2. Gail Sheehy, *Character: America's Search for Leadership* (New York: Morrow, 1988), 15.
3. *Cool Runnings* (Burbank, Calif.: Walt Disney Pictures, 1993).

## Chapter 1: The Bargain of a Lifetime

1. Cited in Robert Andrews, ed., *Famous Lines* (New York: Columbia University Press, 1997), 67.
2. Harper Lee, *To Kill a Mockingbird* (New York: Harper and Row, 1960), 224.
3. F. B. Meyer, *Great Verses Through the Bible: A Devotional Commentary on Key Verses* (Grand Rapids: Zondervan, 1972), 427.
4. Archibald Thomas Robertson, *Word Pictures in the New Testament*, vol. 6 (Nashville: Broadman, 1933), 149.
5. C. S. Lewis, *Mere Christianity* (New York: Macmillan, 1960), 174.
6. Vance Havner, *The Best of Vance Havner* (Grand Rapids: Baker, 1980), 16.
7. *The American Heritage Dictionary of the English Language*, 4th ed. (Boston: Houghton Mifflin, 2000), s.v. "share."
8. Bob Benson, *Come Share the Being* (Nashville: Impact, 1974), 105–6.

## Chapter 2: The Foundation of Faith

1. Cited in Bill and Kathy Peel, *Discover Your Destiny* (Colorado Springs: NavPress, 1996), 54.

2. Cited in Paul W. Powell, *How to Survive a Storm* (Ft. Worth: Annuity Board of the Southern Baptist Convention, 1994), 40.
3. Paul Little, *Faith Is for People* (Santa Ana: Vision House, 1976), 115.
4. Keith Miller and Bruce Larson, *The Edge of Adventure* (Waco: Word, 1974), 29.
5. Cited in David Prior, *Creating Community* (Colorado Springs: NavPress, 1992), 19.

## Chapter 3: Being Moral in an Immoral World

1. Sinclair B. Ferguson, *A Heart for God* (Colorado Springs: NavPress, 1985), 125.
2. William S. Plumer, *Psalms* (1867; reprint, Edinburgh: Banner of Truth Trust, 1975), 557.
3. Author and source unknown.
4. John Murray, *The Epistle to the Romans: The New International Commentary on the New Testament*, vol. 2 (Grand Rapids: Eerdmans, 1965), 114.
5. *The Oxford Dictionary of Quotations*, 3d ed. (Oxford: Oxford University Press, 1980), 550.
6. John Bartlett, ed., *Bartlett's Familiar Quotations* (Boston: Little, Brown & Co., 1980), 560.
7. *Oxford Dictionary of Quotations*, 320.

## Chapter 4: Fostering a Dynamic Relationship with God

1. *The Oxford Dictionary of Quotations*, 3d ed. (Oxford: Oxford University Press, 1980), 282.
2. J. I. Packer, *Knowing God* (Downers Grove, Ill.: InterVarsity, 1973), 13.
3. Ibid., 14–15.
4. John Naisbitt, *Megatrends* (New York: Warner Books, 1984), 17.
5. Cited in Oral Roberts, *A Daily Guide to Miracles* (Tulsa: Pinoak Publications, 1975), 158–59.
6. Anne Ortlund, *Up with Worship* (Ventura: Regal Books, 1975), 22–24.
7. Alan Loy McGinnis, *The Friendship Factor* (Minneapolis: Augsburg, 1979), 37.
8. Robert Boyd Munger, *My Heart—Christ's Home* (Downers Grove, Ill.: InterVarsity, 1986).

9. Sinclair Ferguson, *A Heart for God* (Colorado Springs: NavPress, 1985), 175–76.

10. Ibid., 15.

## Chapter 5: Gaining Control of Your Life

1. Cited in Stephen Donadio, ed., *The New York Public Library Book of Twentieth-Century American Quotations* (New York: Warner Books, 1992), 242.

2. Cited in Sybil Stanton, "Secrets Every Achiever Knows," *Reader's Digest*, September 1987, 63–64.

3. D. G. Kehl, *Control Yourself* (Grand Rapids: Zondervan, 1982), 25.

4. Jerry Bridges, *The Practice of Godliness* (Colorado Springs: NavPress, 1983), 161.

5. Ibid., 161–62. Originally cited in Charles Bridges, *An Exposition of Proverbs* (1846; reprint, Evansville, Ind.: Sovereign Grace Book Club, 1959).

6. Jerry Bridges, *The Practice of Godliness*, 169–70.

7. Elisabeth Elliot, *Discipline: The Glad Surrender* (Old Tappan, N.J.: Revell, 1982), 45.

8. Alan Lakein, *How to Get Control of Your Time and Your Life* (New York: Signet, 1973), 11.

9. Cited in Stanton, "Secrets Every Achiever Knows," 64.

10. M. Scott Peck, *The Road Less Traveled* (New York: Simon and Schuster, 1978), 78.

## Chapter 6: Developing the Art of Perseverance

1. *The Oxford Dictionary of Quotations*, 3d ed. (Oxford: Oxford University Press, 1980), 149–50.

2. *Webster's New Ideal Dictionary*, s.v. "persevere."

3. *Investor's Business Daily*, 9 March 1999, A8.

4. Ray Kroc, *Grinding It Out: The Making of McDonalds* (New York: Berkeley, 1978), 201.

5. Cited in Ted W. Engstrom, *The Pursuit of Excellence* (Grand Rapids: Zondervan, 1982), 51.

6. E. Paul Hovery, *The Treasury of Inspirational Anecdotes, Quotations, and Illustrations* (Old Tappan, N.J.: Revell, 1987), 36.

7. Cited in Ted W. Engstrom, *The Making of a Christian Leader* (Grand Rapids: Zondervan, 1976), 85.

8. Cited in Bill and Kathy Peel, *Discover Your Destiny* (Colorado Springs: NavPress, 1996), 164.
9. Cited in Steven J. Lawson, *Faith Under Fire* (Wheaton: Crossway, 1995), 186.
10. Jack Canfield and Mark Victor Hansen, *A Second Helping of Chicken Soup for the Soul* (Deerfield Beach, Fla.: Health Communications, 1995), 280.

## Chapter 7: Radiating the Aura of Godliness

1. Cited in Douglas L. Fagerstrom and James W. Carlson, *The Lonely Pew* (Grand Rapids: Baker, 1993), 93.
2. Paul W. Powell, *Go-Givers in a Go-Getter World* (Nashville: Broadman, 1986), 17.
3. Charles R. Swindoll, *Improving Your Serve* (Waco: Word, 1981), 52–53.
4. Cited in Craig Brian Larson, ed., *Illustrations for Preaching and Teaching* (Grand Rapids: Baker, 1993), 216.
5. Ibid.
6. Jerry Bridges, *The Practice of Godliness* (Colorado Springs: NavPress, 1983), 18.
7. John Murray, *Principles of Conduct* (Grand Rapids: Eerdmans, 1978), 231.

## Chapter 8: Becoming a More Loving Person

1. Cited in Gary McIntosh and Glen Martin, *Finding Them, Keeping Them* (Nashville: Broadman and Holman, 1992), 95.
2. Cited in Charles R. Swindoll, *The Quest for Character* (Portland: Multnomah Press, 1987), 26.
3. C. S. Lewis, *The Four Loves* (New York: Harcourt, Brace, 1960), 169.
4. Author and source unknown.
5. From a 1782 poem by John Fawcett, "Brotherly Love." It was set the the hymn tune "Dennis" and appeared in its current form in an 1845 hymnal.
6. Erich Fromm, *The Art of Loving* (New York: Harper and Row, 1956), 115.
7. Thomas Dubay, *Caring: A Biblical Theology of Community* (Denville, N.J.: Dimension Books, 1973), 53.
8. Ted Engstrom with Ron Wilson, "The Key to Caring Unconditional Love," *Discipleship Journal*, no. 26 (1985): 24–25.

9. Sue Kidd, *Guideposts* (Carmel, N.Y.: Guideposts Associates, 1979).

10. Alan Loy McGinnis, *The Friendship Factor* (Minneapolis: Augsburg, 1979), 159.

11. Henry Drummond, *The Greatest Thing in the World* (Old Tappan, N.J.: Revell, 1968), 25–27.

12. *The Oxford Dictionary of Quotations*, 3d ed. (Oxford: Oxford University Press, 1979), 578.

13. Kathryn Spink, *The Miracle of Love* (San Francisco: Harper and Row, 1981), 124–25 (emphasis added).

## Chapter 9: Emulating God's Love

1. Oswald Chambers, *My Utmost for His Highest* (New York: Dodd, Mead, 1935), 67.

2. Kenneth S. Wuest, "Bypaths in the Greek New Testament," in *Wuest's Word Studies from the Greek New Testament* (Grand Rapids: Eerdmans, 1973), 110.

3. Source unknown.

4. Bruce Larson, "Out of Line," *Campus Life*, n.d., 47.

5. Cited in James M. Washington, ed., *A Testament of Hope* (San Francisco: Harper/San Francisco, 1986), 256–57.

6. Victor Parachin, "The Mother Teresa Effect," *Christian single*, March 1997, 14.

7. Ellen Weber, "Loving the Unlovely," *Discipleship Journal*, no. 43 (1988): 54.

8. Henry Drummond, *The Greatest Thing in the World* (Old Tappan, N.J.: Revell, 1968), 40, 53.

## Chapter 10: A Toolbox for the Journey

1. Cited in Stephen Donadio, ed., *The New York Public Library Book of Twentieth-Century American Quotations* (New York: Warner Books, 1992), 242.

2. Cited in Robert Boardman, "Only One Thing," *Discipleship Journal*, no. 13 (1983): 18.

3. Donadio, *The New York Public Library Book of Twentieth-Century American Quotations*, 95.

4. *Chariots of Fire* (Burbank, Calif.: Warner Brothers, 1981).

5. William Nicholas, *A New Treasury of Words to Live By* (New York: Simon and Schuster, 1947), 14.

6. *The Oxford Dictionary of Quotations,* 3d ed. (Oxford: Oxford University Press, 1979), 405.
7. William Barclay, *The Letters to the Galatians and Ephesians* (Philadelphia: Westminster, 1976), 100.
8. Ted W. Engstrom, *The Making of a Christian Leader* (Grand Rapids: Zondervan, 1976), 199.

## Chapter 11: A Lifetime Work

1. Bill Hybels, *Who You Are When No One's Looking* (Downers Grove, Ill.: InterVarsity, 1987), 9–10.
2. Ted W. Engstrom, *The Pursuit of Excellence* (Grand Rapids: Zondervan, 1982), 23–24.
3. J. R. Miller, *The Building of Character* (Thomas Y. Crowell Co., 1894).